TRAIN

Your Way to

FINANCIAL

FITNESS

SHANNON McLAY

RIVER GROVE
BOOKS

Published by River Grove Books
Austin, TX
www.greenleafbookgroup.com

Original edition was published under the title
Financially Blonde's Guide to Financial Fitness

Distributed by River Grove Books

For ordering information or special discounts for bulk purchases, please contact River Grove Books at PO Box 91869, Austin, TX 78709, 512.891.6100.

Design and composition by Greenleaf Book Group
Cover design by Greenleaf Book Group
Cover image: ©iStock/whiteisthecolor; ©shutterstock/Robyn Mackenzie

Cataloging-in-Publication data
McLay, Shannon.
  Train your way to financial fitness / Shannon McLay.—Revised edition.
    pages : illustrations ; cm
  Originally published as: Financially blonde's guide to financial fitness. Nicodemos Enterprises, 2013.
  Issued also as an ebook.
  1. Finance, Personal. I. Title.

HG179 .M35 2014
332.024   2014936351

ISBN: 978-1-938416-95-8
eBook: 978-1-938416-96-5

Printed in the United States of America

Revised Edition

This book is dedicated to all those on the journey to financial fitness.

• • •

The road may sometimes be long and difficult,
but never forget to have fun along the way.

CONTENTS

INTRODUCTION

My Financial Fitness Journey

My name is Shannon McLay, and I used to be Financially Fat.

What does that mean? Basically, I was not very smart with my personal finances. The funny thing is, I am a very smart person. I attended and graduated from a top-25 university and while there was accepted into Beta Gamma Sigma, the business honor society open only to the top 7 percent of each business school class. I received five job offers before Thanksgiving of my senior year and accepted an investment banking job that paid well by the standards of a twenty-two-year-old. (In fact, it paid well by the standards of a fifty-two-year-old.) That initial job led to a thirteen-year career in financial services, where I worked with large corporate clients, middle-market companies, hedge fund investors, and ultimately, individual investors. From the outside, it looked as if I had the perfect life and could do no wrong.

Actually, though, I was a mess in many ways; my biggest source of shame was the fact that behind my successful and lucrative career in finance lurked a disastrous personal balance sheet.

. . .

Let me tell you about my journey to discovering that I was Financially Fat. In 2012, at the height of a career with large corporate clients, I made a decision to leave my group and work with retail investors at a well-known wealth management company. Most of my coworkers thought I was crazy; many of those who worked with institutional clients thought it was *beneath* them to work with retail clients. They didn't feel as though retail was as sexy.

However, I had a twofold reason for making this seemingly crazy move at that point in my career. The first was that as I was looking for an adviser myself, I discovered that 80 percent of financial advisers were men. I had been in finance my entire career by this point, and I was frequently the only woman in the room—so this fact wasn't terribly shocking. The second and even more important reason was personal. I was at the point in my financial life when I needed an adviser, and I didn't want it to be a man. If I did not want a male adviser, I was sure there were a number of other people who felt the same.

Don't get me wrong—men are wonderful! I married one, and I birthed one. I enjoy working with men and having them as friends. However, when it came to my personal financial life, I just felt that I couldn't trust a man to handle the complexity of personal finance—for families in particular.

I learned in the wealth management firm that if you were successful in your practice you could build a team, and my intent was to build a team of women and encourage more women to join the ranks of retail financial advisory services.

So I decided to leave and become the adviser that I wanted for myself, while also helping recruit more women to the wealth management profession.

. . .

My time at the retail wealth management firm was some of the most rewarding—and frustrating—of my career. This firm is not a perfect company by any stretch of the imagination, but it excels at supporting and encouraging new advisers. The firm has a three-year training program focused on helping each new adviser develop a successful practice.

While in this program, I believe I learned more than I did in the previous twelve years in finance and two years in business school. I suspected that personal finance was a complex landscape, and I was not wrong. In fact, the training material was so vast that senior advisers would joke that you would feel like you were drinking from a fire hose—truly the perfect analogy for the experience.

What I enjoyed most about the training was that everything I was learning was applicable to me personally or would be applicable to me at a later date. I loved learning about asset allocation, insurance, annuities, and trust and estate planning. And I was successful at what I was doing, so I received a tremendous amount of support from my leadership team, which I enjoyed.

. . .

Drinking from that fire hose taught me many lessons, but the most important one was unintentional. Like most new advisers, I was eager to gain access to "inside information" on the best investments for clients. I assumed that I would learn how to become a market guru who consistently made my clients money by my wise investment choices.

What I learned was that there is no miracle investment. In fact, I sat in many educational meetings with the top brains on Wall Street who all thought they had the best solution; however, at the same time they would express frustrations with the markets, admitting that "they don't make sense."

As I invested clients' monies and watched the rise and fall of fickle markets that seemed to have minds of their own, I realized that these markets were not the answer for my clients.

This epiphany is certainly not something that the wealth management firm intended to teach me, as they have 16,000 advisers and thousands of traders, research analysts, and support staff who would have you believe that the markets mean *everything*. Don't get me wrong; the markets are important. However, they only represent a small part of the picture of financial health.

· · ·

While I was learning my markets lessons, I would provide "wealth analyses" for my clients. To prepare these, I would ask them lots of questions, such as "How much is your salary?" "When do you want to retire?" "How much do you have in your IRA/401K?" "How much income do you think you will need in retirement?" The ultimate goal of the analysis was to take all of their information and see if they were on track for achieving their goals.

When I ran the analysis for clients with the information they provided and with the assumption that they would not change their behavior, *every* client had a less than 15 percent chance of achieving his or her goals. It did not matter if the client was a millionaire or had a mere $100 saved.

With each analysis that I would run, I began to see a little bit of myself in that client, and I found that I was actually afraid to run an analysis on my own family—because I knew that I would not like the results. The fear I felt was something similar to the fear of stepping on a scale when you know that your clothes are tight and you have been eating more than normal. You know that you are probably overweight; however, the second you step on that scale, it will be confirmed to you in black and white. In the same way one might come to the unpleasant realization that he or she is physically fat, I realized that I was Financially Fat.

The discovery of my financial obesity did not scare me too much, though, because when I would begin to "tweak" the numbers for my clients to figure out what they needed to do to achieve their goals, I discovered that if they were ten years or more from retirement, then 100 percent of the time they could achieve *all* of their goals as long as they committed to a savings plan.

Yes, you heard me correctly: *savings*. Changing market performance had little to no impact on their ability to achieve financial success. This discovery was one of the greatest, most valuable lessons that I learned during my intense training period and an important one for me on my financial journey. Just as my clients could change their path to financial success, so could I.

You may remember that earlier I said that my time at the wealth management firm was both rewarding and frustrating. Well, the discovery of the key to the clients' success (and mine) was certainly the most rewarding aspect to me. My frustration at this firm was in my mandate as a financial adviser. I was charged with bringing in new households or families with $250,000 or more in assets. I would technically not get paid for any household with less than that amount.

I understand that this level of wealth is based upon the value the firm put on my time and its resources. However, I was frustrated that all of this training and education would be reserved only for the *wealthy*.

• • •

As I was growing my business, I met many new people along the way, and a number of them asked me to speak with them about their finances. Perhaps because I didn't look or present myself like the other advisers (who were mostly middle-aged men), they felt more comfortable disclosing information to me. I made it a practice to meet with *anyone* who asked me. Despite the fact that the firm wanted me to meet only with people who had a certain amount of money, I was curious to find out what type of help *all* people needed.

This open-door policy led to a number of meetings with those whom I came to call my "pro bonos." These individuals did not have the assets to get the attention and advice of a traditional financial adviser, but they still needed financial help in some way, shape, or form.

By meeting with clients of all income levels, "pro bonos" included, I recognized a common theme that also resonated with me personally: We all needed a road map for living a financially rewarding life—and we didn't know how to create it.

Through my practice, I began to build the road map for my clients and "pro bonos." Each individual, couple, and family is truly a unique entity with distinctive goals and visions for life; therefore, the same road map won't work for everyone. However, despite their unique journeys, the ultimate goal is truly the same for everyone. That is what I call achieving "financial fitness." I created this book based on my experience helping others achieve personal financial fitness.

HOW TO USE THIS BOOK

Even though I work in personal finance, I find most personal finance books tedious and cumbersome. The road to financial fitness may at times become difficult, and the last thing you need is for your guidebook to add to your struggles. This book is designed to be easy to read, with practical applications for your individual personal finance journey. Everyone should read the first chapter, which describes financial fitness and the financial types. Next, you will take a quiz to determine your financial type. The quiz is important for you to complete, because as I mentioned, each road map to financial success is unique, and your financial type helps dictate the best path for you. I advise people that if they get a borderline score on the quiz, they should read the sections for both of their borderline types, as they may find they relate to both. I also advise married couples and those in committed relationships to take the quiz together and then to read their individual section and the one that applies to their significant other, if it is different from their own. To help maintain a healthy relationship, it is important to understand what the other person may need for success and acknowledge the partner's different financial type.

After you take the quiz, you will only read the designated section for your financial type. Each section is written as a single unit, and you will see that some materials are be repeated between sections; the advice may be similar, but the sections are not exactly the same, as each is modified to fit each financial type. Throughout the book there will be exercises to help you strengthen areas of your financial life. Just as you may have exercises that help build your abs or firm your butt, I have provided exercises to tone and firm your finances. After you read your section, you should read the final chapter, which is applicable for all types. Finally, at the end of the book, I have provided the complete list of exercises that you can reference easily as you need them throughout your journey.

As I mentioned earlier, my financial type was Fat. Your score may indicate that you are further on your journey to financial freedom than

I was when I started. However, know that you can change and improve, no matter where you start. You do not need to stay Financially Fat for long. You just need training, tips, and tools to make the right choices, and this book will help you! So, I hope that you sit back, take notes, and commit to making financial fitness a life goal for yourself. And most importantly, enjoy the ride!

CHAPTER 1

What Is Financial Fitness?

In my opinion, next to physical fitness, financial fitness is the number-one key to success in life. I can even argue that it is more important than physical fitness, because poor financial health often leads to the poor physical health associated with stress, high blood pressure, poor nutrition, and so forth. And it is amazing to me that we spend so little time focused on trying to achieve financial fitness. Americans spend millions of dollars a year on gym memberships, diet and weight-loss programs, vitamins, and organic food—all to achieve physical fitness. Yet how many of us say we don't have the time or money to devote to financial fitness?

So what do I mean when I say *financial fitness*? Simply put, it is the state of financial health where you are capable of achieving your financial hopes and dreams. Just as each of us is unique in our life goals, financial fitness does not look and feel the same for everyone. It does not necessarily mean having $1 million in your bank account, having the ability to retire at forty-five, or vacationing at Four Seasons. It could mean those things if you personally desire them, but more generally, financial fitness is the state where you can live the life you want to live and feel comfortable doing it. We frequently get so caught up in what we don't have or what we are not doing that it is difficult for us to understand what type of life we have the means of living.

When I meet with clients and we discuss their life goals and the journey they want to take, part of the meeting involves understanding what the clients want; the other part is explaining to them what they are capable of achieving. A balance between the two does not always exist. If you make $50,000 a year and you are barely able to save any money, then you will likely not be vacationing at Four Seasons. At the same time, if you make $1 million a year and you are barely able to save money, then *you too* should not be vacationing at Four Seasons, no matter how much you think you should.

When I go through the planning process with clients, I typically have the Rolling Stones song "You Can't Always Get What You Want" queued up on my iPod. There is no truer statement when it comes to financial fitness. The first step in attaining it is understanding that you can't always get what you want—meaning that you cannot spend money on your every desire. But that doesn't necessarily mean that you can't have a great life. In fact, when you learn this lesson and plan for financial fitness, you will be happier in the long run.

There are three financial fitness types: Fit, Skinny, and Fat. I will go into more detail on each of these types within their unique sections; however, I will provide you a quick overview here. Just as we should all strive to become physically fit, I believe that we should all strive to become Financially Fit. When you are Financially Fit, you live within your means and plan well for your financial goals. Financially Skinny persons live paycheck to paycheck and feel as though they cannot get ahead, no matter how hard they work. And a Financially Fat person typically overspends and under-saves; this person usually has large amounts of debt relative to earnings.

Before we determine which type you are, let's take the first step to defining what financial success looks like to you . . . which leads us to the first exercise in this book. I encourage you to take the time and thoughtfully perform each exercise. I do these exercises with my clients, and they find them a valuable use of their time.

LIFE'S JOURNEY

When I first meet with clients, I tell them, "Your adult life is like a road trip from New York to California. New York is where you are when you are just starting out, and California is retirement." I view my role as helping them get there:

1. in the time they want to get there;

2. living in the house they want to live in when they get there; and

3. making all of the stops they want to make along the way.

I meet people in all stages of their road trips. Sometimes people are further along in their paths, say in Ohio or Colorado. One of my clients said she felt she was in Maine, because $200,000 in student loan debt had set her back in life. It is not necessarily critical for you to figure out what state you are in. What is more critical at this point is determining what your road trip looks like.

VISUALIZING YOUR JOURNEY

Take five to ten minutes to sit quietly. Close your eyes. Take a few deep breaths and think about what you want out of life. Take a pen and paper and answer as many of these questions as possible.

What is important to you?

1. Do you want to have a career?
2. Do you want to get married?
3. Do you want to have children?
4. Do you want to be a stay-at-home mom or dad?
5. Do you want to retire by a certain age?
6. Do you want to get a college degree or an additional degree?
7. Do you want to buy a house?

What are bucket list items that you absolutely have to do before you die?

1. Do you want to travel internationally?
2. Do you want to skydive?
3. Do you want to give to charity?
4. Do you want to go skiing/hiking/mountain climbing/surfing?

What are everyday things that you feel you need to be happy?

1. Do you like to eat out?
2. Do you like lattés five times a week or more?
3. Do you like to go out with friends multiple times a week?
4. Do you like to go shopping multiple times a month?

The first two lists should be considered your "needs" in life; these are the items that you prioritize when planning.

The third list involves the "wants" you have in life. It is not as critical as the first two, but it would be nice to have these things if you could.

Now look through the lists that you created. Are they long? Short? Looking at the lists, consider the monetary value that each item has. Do you know the value of the items on your list? If not, I highly encourage you to try to determine the value of your wants and needs. This may seem tedious, but it is important to understand the cost of your life's goals. It is especially critical to understand the financial value of your bucket list and absolute *need* list. There are many resources you could utilize to determine the values on your list. For many of the items, www.census.gov has a number of details regarding home costs and potential earnings, and www.ed.gov has great details on educational costs in the US. So if one of your dreams is to purchase a home in Illinois, you would see that the median home price there is $190,000, and if you need 20 percent of the home price as a down payment, then you would need at least $38,000 in cash to achieve this goal in your life.

For more specific goals, I advise clients to research the goal and determine average costs. For example, if you searched "skydiving costs" you would find that the average cost is about $349. So, if skydiving is an important goal for you, you would know that you need to plan for at least $349 to accomplish it.

Now that you have an idea of the value of the wants and needs in your life's journey, it is time to determine whether they are attainable based on what your financial resources are or might be. If you are not able to afford some of these things now, could you afford them later?

Going back to the analogy of the road trip, if you are about to embark on a 3,000-mile trip, won't you save time, money, and energy by using a map or GPS? This first exercise is important in order to understand the stops along the way that you want to make. Now that you have the stops in sight, we can incorporate them into the route. You might be surprised to learn how many of your goals are possible, once you have a plan in place.

Frequently I meet clients who have never gone through this exercise. When we do this together, they realize that they have wasted time and money on nonessential items, which has prevented them from making the stops they truly want to make; now we have to work harder to make those stops a reality for them. It is like driving for days, reaching Indiana, and then realizing you wanted to see Vermont. So now we have to back-track. Wouldn't it have made more sense to see Vermont first?

My clients and I go through this exercise together at least annually. It is important to keep your goals in sight but also to recognize that this list will likely change over time. Life is a long journey, so changes are inevitable. Some changes will be in your control, and others will not. In addition, some plans are near-term, while others may be longer-term.

It is important to acknowledge the near-term events as they approach and focus on those where appropriate. As an example, I have forty-five-year-old clients who have retirement aspirations and education goals for their children. These are their long-term plans. However, they would also like to make an addition to their home in the next two years, which is a short-term goal. Therefore, we are keeping retirement and education constantly in sight while creating a specific plan for the house that will allow them to build the addition within two years without sacrificing those other things.

People who work toward financial fitness are capable of achieving most items on their list. They understand that this yearly list represents what they hope to achieve, and they work to make it a reality. Without the list, how do you know what is important to you? How do you understand the costs? The list is critical to living a Financially Fit life. Again, when you are Financially Fit, achieving the goals on your list will become a reality. Doesn't that sound fun? Don't you want that to be you? Then let's get started!

CHAPTER 2

Financial Fitness Quiz

As I mentioned earlier, we are all unique people with varied goals and values in life. We have all taken different paths that have led us to become the people that we are at this point. While there are many overall personality types, based on my experience with various clients, I believe there are three financial types. I refer to them as *Fit*, *Skinny*, and *Fat*.

Your final score on the following quiz will show you which of these types best describes you. The important thing to note is that *all* types need to work on their financial fitness. Just like physical fitness, financial fitness is an active process. Some of us have to work harder than others; however, all of us need to put in the effort.

During an initial meeting with clients, one of the first things I say to them is "This is a judgment-free zone." And I truly mean it. It is difficult as a planner to help clients if they are not honest with me and, more importantly, if they are not honest with themselves. So I encourage you to take this test and be as honest as you can. If you are not, you will risk being categorized as the "wrong" financial type, and the exercises and goals recommended to you will not be as meaningful or helpful.

As a professional, I can quickly assess a client's financial type after a brief period of time and a review of assets and liabilities. Knowing this information helps me develop the appropriate road map and strategy for helping my clients achieve their personal goals. I have recently formalized the quiz so that readers like you can complete it on their own.

FINANCIAL FITNESS QUIZ

Choose the answer that best describes you or is the closest to how you feel. The point values for your answers are at the end of the quiz.

1. At the end of each pay period after paying your bills you . . .
   - ☐ a. have money left over;
   - ☐ b. have nothing left over but have paid all the bills;
   - ☐ c. have nothing left over and still have other bills to pay.

2. Do you have credit cards?
   - ☐ a. No, I have never applied for one.
   - ☐ b. No, my credit is so bad that I cannot be approved for one.
   - ☐ c. Yes, but I rarely use them.
   - ☐ d. Yes, and I use them all the time.

3. If you answered C or D above, you have . . .
   - ☐ a. one to three credit cards;
   - ☐ b. four to six credit cards;
   - ☐ c. more than six credit cards.

4. Do you have a full-time job?

   ☐ a. Yes, and I am not interested in looking for another one now.

   ☐ b. Yes, but I would be open to finding a new one.

   ☐ c. No, and I am currently looking.

   ☐ d. No, I am retired, still in school, or do not need to work.

5. If you answered A or B above, how would you describe your salary?

   ☐ a. It is fine, and I do not need or want to make more.

   ☐ b. It is below what I would like to make, but enough for now.

   ☐ c. It is below what I would like to make, and not enough for now.

6. I go shopping for things I don't need . . .

   ☐ a. never;

   ☐ b. sometimes;

   ☐ c. all the time.

7. When it comes to investing . . .

   ☐ a. I do not have any money to invest;

   ☐ b. I am not that comfortable, and the markets scare me;

   ☐ c. I am very comfortable with it and enjoy picking my investments.

8. When I go food shopping . . .

    ☐ a. I don't always know what everything costs, but I try to plan what I buy;

    ☐ b. I have no idea how much things cost, I just buy food that looks good when I am there;

    ☐ c. I understand how much everything costs, and I find the best values.

9. When it comes to credit card debt . . .

    ☐ a. I don't have credit card debt;

    ☐ b. I know exactly how much I owe, and I am comfortable with that amount;

    ☐ c. I know how much I owe, and I am not comfortable with that amount;

    ☐ d. I have no idea how much I owe, and I don't look at it.

10. Do you know what your credit score is?

    ☐ a. No, I have never looked at it.

    ☐ b. Yes, it is important to me that I remain creditworthy.

    ☐ c. Yes, and it is below creditworthiness.

11. I eat out . . .

    ☐ a. zero to two times a week;

    ☐ b. three to four times a week;

    ☐ c. five or more times a week.

12. If you wanted to buy a home today, which statement would best describe you?

☐ a. I know how much it costs, and I could afford it.

☐ b. I have no idea how much I would need to buy a home.

☐ c. I know how much it costs, and I could not afford to buy a home in the near future.

13. If you had kids and wanted to send them to college, which statement would best describe you?

☐ a. I know how much it costs, and I could afford it.

☐ b. I have no idea how much it costs to send them to college.

☐ c. I know how much it costs, and I could afford some of it.

☐ d. I know how much it costs, and I could not afford any of it.

☐ e. I think kids should pay for their own college costs.

14. When it comes to student loan debt . . .

☐ a. I have or will have it, and it seems unmanageable;

☐ b. I do not have any, or will not have any;

☐ c. I have or will have some, but I believe it is a manageable amount.

15. When it comes to buying or leasing a car . . .

    ☐ a. I have done it and feel like I planned and got a good deal;

    ☐ b. I have done it, but I didn't plan and feel like I didn't get a good deal;

    ☐ c. I have never done it but I feel like I will be prepared if I do;

    ☐ d. I have never done it but don't need a car;

    ☐ e. I have never done it and have no idea what to do.

16. When it comes to Groupon, Living Social, KGB Deals, or any other daily deal website . . .

    ☐ a. I buy deals all the time and frequently don't use all of them;

    ☐ b. I buy deals more than I should, but I have used all of them;

    ☐ c. I have purchased deals, but they are usually for things I need;

    ☐ d. I have never purchased anything from a deal site.

17. When it comes to shopping for things other than groceries (this could encompass personal care, clothing, transportation, etc.) . . .

    ☐ a. I only do it out of necessity;

    ☐ b. I do it three to four times a week;

    ☐ c. I do it more than four times a week.

18. When I shop for non-food items . . .

    ☐ a. it is planned, and I can afford it;

    ☐ b. it is spontaneous, but I can afford it;

    ☐ c. it is spontaneous, and I can't afford it.

19. When it comes to shopping . . .

    ☐ a. I do not find it difficult to stay away from any store in particular;

    ☐ b. I have a weakness for a store(s) and do not know how to stop myself from going;

    ☐ c. I have a weakness for a store(s), but I can control how frequently I go there.

20. When it comes to retirement . . .

    ☐ a. I have a retirement account and feel like I am prepared for my retirement;

    ☐ b. I have a retirement account but don't feel like I am prepared for my retirement;

    ☐ c. what's a retirement account?

21. When it comes to budgeting . . .

    ☐ a. I have made budgets and stuck to them;

    ☐ b. I have made budgets but couldn't stick to them;

    ☐ c. I have never made a budget but feel like I could stick to one;

    ☐ d. I have never made a budget and don't believe I could live by one.

22. When it comes to online shopping . . .

    ☐ a. I do not find it difficult to avoid shopping online;

    ☐ b. I like to shop online, but I can stop myself if I have to;

    ☐ c. I like to shop online, and I don't know how to stop myself.

23. If I lost my job (or other source of income) tomorrow . . .

    ☐ a. I would have enough money saved to live off of for six months or more;

    ☐ b. I would have enough money saved to make it one to six months;

    ☐ c. I would not have enough money saved to last a month.

24. When it comes to health insurance . . .

    ☐ a. I have health insurance and do not have an issue paying for it;

    ☐ b. I have health insurance, but it is a challenge to pay for it;

    ☐ c. I do not have health insurance, and I could not afford to pay for it.

25. When it comes to emailed coupons or discounts . . .

    ☐ a. I look for and use coupons or online discounts for things I need;

    ☐ b. I use coupons or online discounts just because I have them, even if I don't need the things I buy;

    ☐ c. I never use coupons or online discounts.

· · ·

Following are the point values for your answers to the quiz. Total your points. The applicable fitness types are below, based on your total score.

1. At the end of each pay period after paying your bills you . . .
   - ☐ a. 1
   - ☐ b. 5
   - ☐ c. 10

2. Do you have credit cards?
   - ☐ a. 4
   - ☐ b. 10
   - ☐ c. 1
   - ☐ d. 7

3. If you answered C or D above, you have . . .
   - ☐ a. 1
   - ☐ b. 5
   - ☐ c. 10

4. Do you have a full-time job?
   - ☐ a. 1
   - ☐ b. 5
   - ☐ c. 10
   - ☐ d. 2

5. If you answered A or B above, how would you describe your salary?
   - ☐ a. 1
   - ☐ b. 5
   - ☐ c. 10

6. I go shopping for things I don't need . . .

☐　a. 1

☐　b. 5

☐　c. 10

7. When it comes to investing . . .

☐　a. 10

☐　b. 5

☐　c. 1

8. When I go food shopping . . .

☐　a. 5

☐　b. 10

☐　c. 1

9. When it comes to credit card debt . . .

☐　a. 1

☐　b. 4

☐　c. 8

☐　d. 10

10. Do you know what your credit score is?

☐　a. 5

☐　b. 1

☐　c. 10

11. I eat out . . .

    ☐ a. 1

    ☐ b. 5

    ☐ c. 10

12. If you wanted to buy a home today, which statement would best describe you?

    ☐ a. 1

    ☐ b. 5

    ☐ c. 10

13. If you had kids and wanted to send them to college, which statement would best describe you?

    ☐ a. 1

    ☐ b. 10

    ☐ c. 4

    ☐ d. 6

    ☐ e. 7

14. When it comes to student loan debt . . .

    ☐ a. 10

    ☐ b. 5

    ☐ c. 1

15. When it comes to buying or leasing a car . . .

   ☐ a. 1

   ☐ b. 10

   ☐ c. 2

   ☐ d. 3

   ☐ e. 7

16. When it comes to Groupon, Living Social, KGB Deals, or any other daily deal website . . .

   ☐ a. 10

   ☐ b. 5

   ☐ c. 1

   ☐ d. 3

17. When it comes to shopping for things other than groceries . . .

   ☐ a. 1

   ☐ b. 5

   ☐ c. 10

18. When I shop for non-food items . . .

   ☐ a. 1

   ☐ b. 5

   ☐ c. 10

19. When it comes to shopping...

    ☐ a. 1

    ☐ b. 10

    ☐ c. 5

20. When it comes to retirement...

    ☐ a. 1

    ☐ b. 5

    ☐ c. 10

21. When it comes to budgeting...

    ☐ a. 1

    ☐ b. 5

    ☐ c. 4

    ☐ d. 10

22. When it comes to online shopping...

    ☐ a. 1

    ☐ b. 5

    ☐ c. 10

23. If I lost my job (or other source of income) tomorrow...

    ☐ a. 1

    ☐ b. 5

    ☐ c. 10

24. When it comes to health insurance . . .

☐ a. 1

☐ b. 5

☐ c. 10

25. When it comes to emailed coupons or discounts . . .

☐ a. 1

☐ b. 10

☐ c. 5

RESULTS:

If you scored between 25–50, you are Financially Fit and you should read chapters 3 and 6.

If you scored between 51–125, you are Financially Skinny and you should read chapters 4 and 6.

If you scored between 126–250, you are Financially Fat and you should read chapters 5 and 6.

Please note that if you were scored as Financially Fit and you received a 10 on any of the following questions—1, 2, 6, 8, 9, 10, 17, 18, 19, 22, or 23—then I think you may need help in certain areas. It may make sense for you to read the Financially Skinny chapter as well. If you scored on the high end of your range, then I would consider you "borderline" and advise that you read your chapter and the following one.

CHAPTER 3

Financially Fit

Congratulations! Of the three financial types, yours is probably the "easiest to train." In fact, you are so very good with your finances that I am sure you are curious what type of training you actually need. My experience with clients suggests that no matter what their financial type, everyone needs to work not only to achieve financial fitness but also to maintain it. So let's consider in greater depth the types of financial decisions you make and how training can help you achieve your financial goals even faster.

You are basically the "saver." You understand the importance of phrases like "living within your means," and your friends probably call you "cheap" or "frugal." In some sense all of these titles probably fit, but there is nothing wrong with that. When I see Fit clients, the biggest financial challenges they have are:

1. spending money;

2. using credit;

3. and investing wisely.

SPENDING MONEY

For whatever reason, you have always known that it is better to save than to spend. From an early age, you probably had no issue with staying at home on a Friday night rather than going out with friends if you didn't have the money. Most Fit people experienced financial hardships at some point in their early lives, and those hardships left a lasting impression and a desire never to feel that way again. In fact, many would do just about anything—including forsaking happiness, convenience, or living a hermit lifestyle—not to experience financial hardship again.

Many people who grew up during the Depression are this financial type. For fit people, saving and not spending is such a core value that they have a difficult time understanding why others "don't get it," and they are almost prejudiced against those who do spend.

An important step to achieving financial fitness for you is to understand that spending is okay. In fact, spending money on important items and people will make you a happier person. If you are employed, I am sure that you work hard. It is important for you to realize that your hard work not only can provide you with a safety net and cushion, but it can also bring you happiness and release. When we do good things for other people not because they asked or because we expect anything back in return, we truly find the ultimate sense of happiness.

I am not telling you to go out and buy your friends and family homes or Porsches or anything like that; however, I challenge you to spend money on more "fun" things than you have in the past. Again, this may be a difficult thing for you to do, and perhaps after you spend money often you have buyer's remorse. So I challenge you to plan for your spending.

Think about something you have always wanted to do or something that someone you love *really* wants. Your initial thought is probably that this item or experience is "frivolous"; however, I challenge you to put one or two of these things in your plan every year and follow through on them.

I have a client who is Fit. She is in her mid-forties and has never married or had children. She is very conservative in her spending and has a good cushion should anything negative happen to her career. However, she lives a very isolated lifestyle; she avoids going out with friends or coworkers because she does not want to "waste her money." She has expressed that she would like to engage in more social activities; however, she is truly afraid to spend her money in case a financial catastrophe occurs.

She recently decided to take an international trip with her sister. This was a *huge* step for her. She did not want to spend the money (even though she had it), but it was a rare opportunity that surfaced, and she felt that she should take the risk. The trip ended up being one of the highlights of her life to date. She had fun with her sister and friends, but more importantly, she had a unique life experience that she never would have had from the comfort of her living room sofa.

I frequently see Fit clients get what I call "saver's fatigue" because they have not given themselves an outlet to spend the money they are saving. The following is a good exercise if you feel as though you may succumb to saver's fatigue.

SPENDING MONEY

Sit down and think of two ways you can spend money. The first is on something for you. You do not have to go crazy, but think about something you have always wanted to do——and do it! The other involves doing something for someone else. Think about a way you can surprise a person you love with a long-desired thing or experience. For my clients who have spending goals such as these, we usually set up a separate savings account for "fun" money. Some clients determine in advance how much fun money they will need and make a specific savings objective for it. For example, if they want to take a trip and the trip costs $500, they plan to put $42 a month in this account so that after a year, they will have the $500 saved. Other clients use this account for leftover money they have at the end of the month. They know that it is not earmarked for any emergencies or necessities, so if they want to use the money for fun, they have available whatever is in that account. The fun money account is a great method for spending money while not feeling bad about it. My clients like knowing that they have planned for fun.

USING CREDIT

Most Fit people I know have few or no credit cards. This is not because they cannot get approved for them; rather, they think that credit cards create more problems than they solve. Fit people typically pay with cash, debit cards, or checks. They like to know definitively that they have the money they are spending. If they can't pay for something at that exact moment, then they feel that they should not buy the item.

It does not matter if the purchase is a large or a small one. I have a Financially Fit friend who actually purchased his home entirely in cash.

While I applaud the restraint and fiscal responsibility that paying in cash represents, there are many benefits to using credit. Instead of using cash all of the time, you should stop and think about a credit alternative. Let's explore a few of those benefits.

INTEREST EARNED ON YOUR MONEY

Typically when you purchase something with credit, you have at least thirty days until you have to pay the credit card company. Take for example a $1,000 purchase. If you were going to pay cash for this item, the cash would come out of your checking account immediately. If you utilized a credit card, though, you would have an additional thirty days of this cash sitting in your bank account.

If your bank paid you 5 percent on your cash, and if you had $1,000 in the bank, this would amount to a little over $4 for the month. You may think that sounds like a small amount of money, but I bet if you found $4 on the street you would be excited about it. Why not find it in your own bank account? I always tell clients that interest paid to you by banks is "free money."

The relatively small size of the interest earned does not change the fact that it is free, and you should value it as such. If you are looking at a purchase of this size or larger from a store that offers free financing for a period of time, then the same rule applies. Plus, you get even more time to earn free money. If you were going to spend the same $1,000 and got free financing for twelve months, then this would mean that you had twelve months for your money to earn interest for you. At 5 percent, you are now looking at $50 for the year. Now imagine if you found $50 on the street!

These strategies obviously only work if you plan to pay the credit card company back before interest and penalties are charged on the credit cards. My clients make sure that they give themselves reminders with plenty of time before the due date so that they do not incur undue penalties with this strategy.

POINTS/REWARDS AND CASH BACK

Many companies offer cards that give you points, rewards, or cash back on money that you spend on the card. This is another way that you can get free money, this time from the credit card company. Depending on the card, on average, you can expect to get 1 percent back on what you spend or 1 percent toward points or rewards.

Going back to the $1,000 purchase, this would mean for every $1,000 you spend, you would get a $10 value in either cash or rewards. If you were already planning on spending this money, then why not get rewarded for doing so?

There are many types of rewards cards, and I always advise clients to utilize the ones that would provide the most meaningful benefits. I have a client who only flies on Southwest Airlines and likes to travel. So she utilizes the Southwest credit card, and her spending helps pay for her trips. Because she is earning points on money she was going to spend anyway, we can put it to work elsewhere at the same time. I have some clients who like to give money to charity, and there are a number of cards that will let you do just that.

I know a number of people who also take advantage of the sign-up bonus on rewards cards, where if you spend a certain amount of money on the card in a given period, you will be given extra rewards and points. This is a great strategy to utilize when you know you have a large impending purchase.

The only catch with rewards cards is the possibility of an annual fee, which is how many of these card companies fund their rewards programs. Depending on the rewards level, the fee may be reasonable. If your annual fee were $100, then you would be paying around $8 a month for the benefit of using this card. As long as your rewards are more than $8 a month, then the fee makes sense. So, if you spend $1,000 a month and get $10 back, $8 would go to the fee and $2 would be your truly free money.

If you cannot easily determine the annual fee on the rewards card, call the company and ask. Look for rewards cards with no annual fee as well, or for card companies that will give you the first year free.

IMPROVED CREDIT SCORE

As a Financially Fit person, you have made good financial decisions, so you probably already have an above-average credit score; however, credit scores are always improved by actually using credit. The more you responsibly use credit cards, the more you improve your credit score. I recently met with a Financially Fit person who had a lower than expected credit score based on the fact that she did not have many credit cards. It does feel like a Catch-22, but the more credit you have and the more you use it, the better your credit score will be.

FLEXIBILITY IN CASE OF EMERGENCY

When you use credit, you free up your cash for other purposes, especially emergencies. Nowadays almost all merchants take credit cards for payment; however, these cannot always be used for everything. At the end of the day, cash is king, and it will remain so unless we have some global financial meltdown that requires us to start trading in gold, goods, and services again. Until that day, it is always wise to keep a responsible reserve of cash for emergencies.

It is important to note that when I mention using credit, I don't always mean credit cards. Let's go back to the example of my wonderful friend who purchased his house with cash. He saved and worked hard for years to build up enough money to pay for his house and closing costs. The only problem with this strategy is that after he closed, he realized that his home needed some substantial repairs, and he did not have enough cash left in his reserves to pay for them. He ultimately was able to obtain a home equity line on his home to cover these repairs. The good news for him is that, as with a mortgage, he is able to deduct the interest he pays on his home equity line of credit from his tax return. The bad news is that he has less overall credit available (home equity lines are typically smaller than mortgages), and he has the possibility of paying more interest over time, depending on the type of home equity line he utilized.

As I frequently tell clients, their financial journey is a long one, and despite all of the planning you can do, you never know what unexpected situations can arise. Like a spare tire, a cash reserve is the best way to plan for those unexpected events on your life's journey. The optimal size of your cash reserve depends on many factors. When I have clients who intend to buy a home, we plan on a cash reserve for their down payment and closing costs, but I always make sure that they have four to six months of mortgage payments reserved and another reserve for repairs, especially if they are buying an older home. No matter how great your home inspector is or how reliable you think the previous owners are, you never know what issues may be lurking in your "used" home.

A bank or mortgage provider requires you to have enough cash for the down payment and closing costs, but they do not demand that you have cash beyond those figures (they primarily look at your income as an indicator of repayment after closing). Remember, a bank or mortgage company is just a pit stop on your journey through life, and they are not really concerned with you beyond that one initial stop. I want to see you have the ability to make *all* of the stops you would like to make.

There are many opinions on how to manage the types of credit that you have, and I encourage you to constantly compare what interest rates you are paying across these types of credit options. I sometimes see clients with balances on credit cards with interest rates of 15–20 percent; however, they have or could have a home equity line of credit that they could utilize to pay down the credit cards and pay less than 6 percent. On $10,000, this could save you $900 a year. Using credit like mortgages, credit cards, or home equity lines may result in some interest payments that you did not want to make. However, they give you more freedom with your cash, which could be worth more than that down the road.

USE YOUR CREDIT CARD MORE

If you are someone who *rarely* uses your credit card, I challenge you to start using it more. Think about the times when you use your debit card or pay with a check and determine whether you can change your payment method to a credit card. For every time that you use the card, keep your receipt and do not pay the card right away. Wait until your credit card payment date and then pay the bill. If you make a practice of this strategy and it becomes part of your routine, you will earn more money in your checking or savings accounts, and you can earn points and rewards, depending on your card type.

INVESTING WISELY

Most Financially Fit people are very conservative when it comes to investing. They do not take like to take risks with their money, and they view investment accounts as risks. I have mentioned before that I became disillusioned with the attempt to predict the performance of financial markets while I worked at the wealth management firm, but I still find value in them. I believe that over time, and with a well-diversified portfolio that is rebalanced at least once a year, you can achieve 6–8 percent returns. There are risks to achieving this performance; however, I feel that it is a good and achievable estimate.

Those of us who had money invested in stocks from 2000 to 2012 find it difficult to believe that there is much value in the financial markets. And when you look at stocks over this period of time, that assessment is pretty much true. The stock market was basically flat during this time, meaning that if you invested $100 in 2000, you would have $100 in 2012. Some people reading this may even have lost money in the markets at this time. There were a number of significant drops in stocks, but there were significant gains as well. The issue with performance in people's investment portfolios over this period of time was not the fact that they were invested in stocks; it is that they were invested in *too much* stock and not in enough other investments.

While stocks did not perform well in recent years, the bond market did. If you have a well-diversified portfolio, meaning you invested in stocks *and* bonds, then you had better returns than someone who did not.

When you make any investment with your money, there are always risks; however, it is important to understand the types of money you have and what is appropriate for each money type. I always tell my clients that they have three buckets of money: cash, "moon" money, and "life" money.

Cash is the money that you might need for living expenses within the next six months to a year (depending on how conservative you are) should any catastrophic life event happen, such as a job loss or death of a spouse. Cash should typically be kept in a bank, savings account, or money market mutual fund—i.e., very conservative investments that are available to you daily. You want to take minimal risk with this money, as it represents your emergency funds.

Moon money represents the funds that you will need to draw during retirement. I call it moon money because if you are under 59½ years old or more than ten years from retirement, this is money that you should not touch. When you think of accessing it, consider it as easy to reach as the moon. Moon money should be invested the most aggressively. You have time until your retirement, so these funds can fluctuate up and down with the markets. Over time, they will make you more money than your bank account, despite the fact that sometimes it does not feel like it.

That leaves us with life money. This is the money that you have saved that allows you to live the life you want by doing things like buying a home or going on vacation. This money gives you the most flexibility to live your life. And many clients, especially Fit people, believe that this money should be treated as cash and exposed to no risk whatsoever. I understand this thought process. This is the money that is reserved for "life," and no one wants his or her life to be at risk. However, if you do not plan to utilize this money in the next two to five years, then it should not be sitting in a checking account. It should not be invested as aggressively as the moon money, but it should be invested in something more aggressive than a bank account. As the time comes closer to using the money, it should be moved into the cash bucket. Until then, it should be working for you by earning interest or growing in value.

I had clients who kept a significant amount of money (greater than $50,000) in a checking account. They only needed a small portion of this money for cash and emergencies; therefore, we invested the remainder in bond funds. These are more risky than a bank account and could lose value on any given day; however, over a period of two to five years, they will earn more money than a bank account.

Since you are Financially Fit, you have been good with saving and you probably have money in each of your three buckets, but you probably don't realize that each one should be progressively riskier. When you separate the three and invest wisely, your buckets will grow over time with minimal effort on your part.

BUCKETS

Reserve some time in your calendar to review your money and where you have it invested or deposited. Look at the total picture and determine whether you have three buckets (cash, life money, and moon or retirement money) or just one or two. If you have fewer than three, determine which bucket needs more. If you have three buckets, review what they are invested in. If they are too conservative, think about ways to take on more risk. You can speak to a financial adviser or consult with any number of financial websites like ETrade, Fidelity, Vanguard, or Charles Schwab.

INVESTMENTS

If you realized that the investments in your life or moon buckets are too conservative, you need to take some time to educate yourself on taking proper investment risk. Most of my clients who are not investing as much as they should are typically not doing it because they are afraid of the unknown. They have not had enough education on investing.

I know that for some people, investing money seems incredibly scary and complicated—I was one of those people. However, with some education and practice, it really is not that painful. The first resource I tell clients to utilize is their own investment firm. If you already have a retirement account or brokerage account with ETrade, Fidelity, or any other firm, you should feel free to use their resources. After all, your balances are making them money, so you should feel free to benefit in return. Many of these websites have great online classes and tutorials, or you can always call their 800 numbers and speak to an adviser. If you choose to speak with an adviser, make sure that this person explains concepts to you until you understand them. I hate to see people invest in things and not fully understand them because they were afraid to ask questions. Ask lots of questions! It's your money, and you deserve to feel completely comfortable with what you do with it.

I also think there are a number of great blogs out there that explain investing in a very useful manner. Just by searching "finance blogs," you will discover quite a number. I have recently started a YouTube channel where I discuss various investment topics. I encourage you to check it out.

Just as it takes time to get physically fit, it takes time to gain an understanding of investments; however, it is time that is very well spent, in my opinion. I encourage you to dedicate time in your calendar to finding the investment resources that most appeal to you and then spending some time each week reviewing them. Once you have gone through the exercise of determining your money buckets and how much should be put in each, it will be a matter of determining the best asset allocation for each bucket. When you are researching your investment options, look for those that will meet your asset allocation needs. Generally speaking, your cash bucket should have a conservative asset allocation, your life bucket options should be moderately conservative to moderate, and your moon bucket options should be moderately aggressive to aggressive. Knowing your appropriate asset allocation actually makes the selection of investments a much easier process. And again, many financial websites provide guidance on what asset allocation might be best for you, based on your life goals.

CHAPTER 4

Financially Skinny

At first, you were probably excited to see your type; after all, who doesn't want to be skinny? From a financial perspective, though, Skinny people have a number of challenges. I call this type "Skinny" because you literally live paycheck to paycheck, and you are barely getting by financially. Just as it is not good for your body to be deprived of food, it is not good to deprive your bank account of cash. You have a difficult time saving and getting ahead because of various challenges in your financial life.

You probably have the most difficult personality type to get Financially Fit. I liken the financial fitness process of a Financially Skinny person to the effort of trying to lose the last five pounds out of fifty during a weight-loss plan. The first forty-five are the "easy" pounds, while the last five take more work, energy, and strategy. At the same time, you are not too far away from your goals; therefore, even though it may be hard work, you should not have to do it as consistently or as vigorously as your Financially Fat friend. Financially Skinny people need to focus on the details during their journey to financial fitness. The steps that you will need to take to become Financially Fit include:

1. pulling out the fine-tooth comb;

2. categorizing your spending;

3. finding your problem areas;

4. creating your "FitPlan";

5. committing to the plan.

PULL OUT THE FINE-TOOTH COMB

My Financially Skinny clients typically tell me that they "can't save money" and that they "live paycheck to paycheck." If you are not paying attention to the details, then those statements are absolutely correct. However, when I hear these claims, the first thing I tell them to do is open up their credit card and bank account statements. We typically review at least three to four months' worth of statements so that we can pick up any patterns or recurring items over that period of time.

From this point, we go through the statements with a fine-tooth comb. We evaluate and discuss *every single purchase*. This process may seem tedious and useless; however, you would be shocked at how many "little" items add up to something significant over time. I frequently have clients who have recurring charges on their cards that they didn't realize were there. I was one of those people myself. When I took out the fine-tooth comb, I realized that I was paying $9 a month for one credit-reporting agency and $14.95 for another to do the same thing. I was obsessed with my credit report for a while, convinced that someone was going to steal my credit information and ruin my score. Singularly, these charges did not mean much of a hardship for me. Combined, though, they represented almost $300 a year. Now, I love my credit score, but $300 could mean a lot more fun things—like shoes!

Other clients didn't realize how much their latté habit was costing them. Four dollars a day does not seem like much on its own. But over five days that is $20; over the course of a month, it is $80; and over the course of a year, it is $960. Do not think that I am bashing lattés or other small indulgences. I personally have a latté habit that is a daily ritual I would not give up for anything in the world—so I have planned for it. But if you could drink coffee at work or at home instead, $960 is a great bonus you can give yourself fairly easily.

When you are Skinny, it is important to scrutinize every single purchase and spending habit that you have. One time I was going through the process with a client, and we realized that she was paying car insurance for a car she rarely drove. When we really analyzed the value of the insurance, we realized that it was an unnecessary expense that she could suspend until she used the car again. This decision added $1,200 to her bank account that year.

Sometimes we convince ourselves that our spending is necessary; however, when we take the time to truly consider, we start to realize that maybe some of the things we are doing are not so much necessary as just habits that we can live without.

If you have a difficult time questioning your spending habits, then I encourage you to invite a friend over and have him or her help you analyze the value of your purchases. Preferably this friend should be Financially Fit or Skinny, and not Fat, in order to be best equipped to help you analyze your spending objectively.

USING THE FINE-TOOTH COMB

Print out three to four months of credit and debit card statements. Yes,
print them out! I find that people are able to analyze information better
when it is in print. Then look at the expenses in order of size value and
categorize them by high, medium, and low costs. Then look at the frequency
of each purchase. Do you see multiple charges for one location? Do you see
daily or weekly charges for something? Is this a good thing or a bad thing?
We will use this analysis in a later exercise.

CATEGORIZE YOUR SPENDING

In order to determine the problem areas to target, you need to organize
your spending into three categories: needs, wants, and wastes. A *need*
is an expense that you truly cannot live without. Items in this category
would include rent or mortgage, insurance payments, and any other
debt payments that you are obligated to make, such as student loan
debt and car payments. A *want* is something that you desire, but you
can typically find a more cost-effective alternative. Examples might
include food, gas, phone, and entertainment. And *wastes* are just as
you would imagine; they do not typically create much value in your
life, and purchasing them takes you further from your financial goals.
Examples of wastes are clothes, shoes, apps, games, and so forth.

The importance of the three categories is that many people often
think that wants fall into their needs category. Again, needs are any
fixed costs that you absolutely have to pay. After that, most items
should fall into wants or wastes. I tell clients that food is a want because

there are many ways that you can include food in your spending other than the way that you likely currently achieve it. Eating out for all three meals every day is not the most cost-effective method for feeding yourself. If you are living paycheck to paycheck, then this is an easy area to start to fix right away. I used to fall into the trap of eating out too much; however, I was able to take control of my eating behaviors. I planned my shopping better and cut my food costs by 70 percent, just by changing the way I ate.

I also have a number of clients who *love* eating organic food. I like organic food, but do you really need to eat certain types of food in organic form? When you truly analyze the value of organic, you will discover that it is not a necessity in certain areas. You are just falling prey to very compelling marketing. An organic lifestyle is a want, not a need, in my mind. The fact is that organic foods could cost 50 to 100 percent more than their traditional counterparts. If you are spending $100 a week for food, you could potentially reduce that to $50 and save yourself $200 a month by lessening your organic consumption.

I don't want anyone to think that I am bashing organic food or the natural living industry. Rather, I mention organic food because I am concerned about your financial health, and I frequently see clients make themselves financially unhealthy in an effort to make themselves physically healthy. If you can afford to pay 50 to 100 percent more for organic food and you have planned for it, then I am supportive of that strategy. However, if you cannot afford to eat 100 percent organic, then do more research into the value of organic food. Or limit yourself to those few items that are deemed necessary to avoid directly consuming pesticides and other harmful ingredients.

Another want often confused for a need is gas expenses for your car. Fuel prices are challenging for everyone who drives; however, sometimes driving (or at least driving alone) is not the only way that you can get where you need to go. I know that mass transit may not be appealing to you or may not be the most convenient method of transportation; however, if you could use it as an alternative to driving in certain circumstances, you could save yourself money on your gas costs. I also like to see clients try carpooling with their significant other or coworkers. Again, this may add some inconvenience or extra time to your schedule; however, in the process of achieving financial fitness, you will find that there are a number of "inconveniences" that will reap financial rewards for you down the road.

Just as wants can be confused with needs, many wastes are confused for wants or needs. I imagine that you have viewed many of these items as a need or a want. You will say, "Shannon, I *needed* to get a new phone." Or, "Shannon, I *needed* new clothes for work." You may *think* that you needed these things, and maybe you truly did. But could you have made better choices, instead of overspending and putting them in the waste category? I typically view wastes as purchases that set you further behind in achieving your financial goals. When you are looking at your waste items, a good rule of thumb is to ask yourself if the purchase helped or hurt you in reaching your financial goals. If it hurt you, then you know it belongs in the waste category. Later in the book, we are going to discuss putting your plan in place, and if you truly need some of these items and you plan for them, then it will not have been money wasted in your pursuit of financial fitness. However, if you did not plan for these items, then it is exactly the same as throwing your money in the garbage.

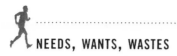

NEEDS, WANTS, WASTES

Review your spending from the last three to four months (you can use your information from the fine-tooth comb exercise) and try to place every dollar spent into one of these categories. If you have everything listed as a need, then you should go back and look at each item more objectively or ask for help in categorizing everything. Look at your wastes and add them up. How much could you have saved in three to four months if you had avoided wastes? Are there wants or wastes that can be eliminated or adjusted?

FIND YOUR PROBLEM AREAS

After going through the fine-tooth comb and "needs, wants, wastes" exercises, did you determine what I call "problem areas"? These represent continual spending behaviors that can be corrected. Problem areas are easy to find, because they will appear multiple times in your bank and credit card statements. A car payment or mortgage payment would not be a problem area, and not all problem areas can be completely resolved; however, the first step is acknowledging they exist so that you can determine whether there is a way to control them.

For example, when I started Weight Watchers, I knew that McDonald's was a problem area for me. Lacking self-control, I could not go there and order a salad or something that was low in Weight Watchers points. However, because I knew McDonald's was a problem area, I could create a plan to avoid it or manage it better. Similarly, I had a client who had a clothing store show up on her credit card statement more times than it should in any given month. Don't get me wrong—I love clothes shopping as much as the next person. However, this is not the type of store that should appear on your credit card statement more than a food store or gas station. We immediately knew this was a problem area for her and could deal with it accordingly.

Other problem areas that sometimes take work to consolidate include going out to eat and recreation. One charge for Capital Grille does not seem like much, but when you take Capital Grille, Houston's, Applebee's, and PF Chang's and add them together, it becomes a problem area. For young people in bigger cities, this typically happens with bars. I have a client who frequently does not know where she has been except by reviewing her debit card statement.

Gas purchases are an often-concealed problem area. Most of us rarely go to the same station every time we fill up, so there could be multiple names that you have to identify and aggregate to determine whether this is a problem area for you to work on.

You may think all of this examination and consolidation is a waste of time, or you will tell me that there are budget programs like Mint.com that will point out these things for you. And it is true that some of these programs can consolidate information. However, none are perfect, and you will typically discover that you have a large number of expenses called "uncategorized" because the program does not know whether the location was a gas station or a restaurant. This uncategorized category prevents the eye-opening experience of truly seeing where your money goes. Most of my clients do not realize that they frequent places as often as they do or that they spend as much money as they do in certain areas.

Identifying problem areas is a huge step in achieving financial fitness. Sometimes we do not even realize that they are problems until we sit and analyze our spending. Once we know that they are keeping us from becoming Financially Fit, then we can find solutions to help us manage them so that they are less problematic.

TARGET AND ATTACK PROBLEM AREAS

If you have determined any problem areas above, write them down and strategize on how to eliminate or work on them. Consider whether each is a problem because of the frequency of purchases, the size of purchases, or both. Do you really need to go to Starbucks every day? Can you replace one of those Starbucks trips with coffee from home or a cart on the street? Are you going to J. Crew or any retail store too much? Determine why you are frequenting the store. Is it because it is on your way home? Can you plan a different way home? Can you walk into the store, find things you would want to buy, write down the prices, and simply walk out? If you are spending too much money on gas, is there another mode of transportation that you can take to save money? It is important to create specific plans for how you will overcome problem areas in your spending. Otherwise, they will continue to remain problems.

SPENDING——*STOP* AND *WHY*

Most people have spending problems at various times in their life. Some of us have it worse than others. I had a *very* bad spending problem that stemmed from making good money and having access to credit. I always told myself there would be more money down the road, so I could put purchases on my credit card. I *never* thought there would be an end to the money. However, when I wanted to make a career change that would provide me less money but more fulfillment, I realized that I needed to control my spending. The basic tenets of financial health are earning more and spending less. If you cannot earn more, then you need to spend less. This exercise is the most valuable for helping my clients with their spending, and you can do it *every single day*. Every time you are about to spend money, STOP yourself for a brief minute and ask WHY? Why are you buying what you are buying?

The great news for you is that there are only two correct answers to this question: (1) It is life and death. You will literally die if you don't buy health insurance or a medication or take a trip to the emergency room; (2) you have planned for it. If you made that purchase of the new phone or the clothes for work part of your plan for the year, then you can go ahead and buy that item. If one of these two answers was not applicable, put down that item, walk away, and don't look back.

THE FOLLOW-UP TO *STOP* AND *WHY*

So you have just practiced the STOP and WHY exercise, and you feel bad. You typically feel good buying things and spending money and you *really* wanted to spend the money you were just going to—but instead you practiced a financial fitness exercise, and now you feel bad. Now what? When you experience this level of sadness for not making a purchase, find a new outlet for the displaced happiness.

When I was losing weight, I really wanted to eat a cheeseburger. Eating a salad just didn't feel as good. So I would eat the salad and visualize the way it would make me look. Or I would let myself have a small treat with the salad, such as a glass of wine or a piece of candy. Similarly, the thing you were just about to buy was not part of your plan, but is there something else that is? Can you buy that instead?

You can also try distracting yourself with something that makes you happy. Call a friend, play an app on your phone, go for a walk. Try a number of different distracting exercises so that you do not fixate on the fact that you feel bad that you did not make that purchase. You do not want to feel as though you are deprived or missing out while you are on the road to financial fitness. If you do, then you are less likely to stay on this important path.

NO-SPEND DAYS

Another way to prevent yourself from having a spending issue is to commit to achieving a certain number of "no-spend" days a month. During a no-spend day, you literally will plan to not use your cash, debit cards, or credit cards for an entire day. It is a best practice to plan one of these a week, and an easy way to accomplish this exercise is just to take your driver's license out with you and leave the rest of your wallet home for the day. While you are practicing a no-spend day, make sure you reflect on where you would have spent money if you could have spent money. This is another great way for you to identify problem areas in your spending life.

CASH-ONLY DAYS

Similar to no-spend days, I think it is a best practice to have at least one cash-only day a week. The set amount of cash you allow yourself to spend during the day should be a difficult goal for you, and for most clients this number is usually around $20. Think of cash-only days like your "push days" when you are working out at the gym. Maybe you can easily run two miles at a time, but on a push day, you make yourself run three. Maybe you normally spend $40 a day on various items, so push yourself once a week to only spend $20.

CREATE YOUR FITPLAN

At this point, you have gone through three to four months of spending with a fine-tooth comb, categorized your spending, and determined where your problem areas are. Now you need to determine what you are going to do about them. This is when we establish the fitness plan, or "FitPlan." The number one reason for my clients becoming Skinny or Fat is the lack of having a plan in place. Traditionally this plan is called a budget. Personally, I think that "budget" is another "four-letter word," like "diet." No one (except maybe a Fit person) likes the idea of living on a budget, so they choose not to. The truth is, we actually don't need a budget; we need a plan.

Going back to the road-trip analogy, doesn't it make more sense to plot out the trip on GPS or a map rather than get in a car and just drive? Without a FitPlan, this is exactly what we do every day in our financial lives, and then we wonder why we have overspent or live paycheck to paycheck. If we can plan for as much of our life as possible, then we are not limiting ourselves as we imagine we would be doing on a budget or diet. Instead, we are making a lifestyle change that will actually help us get what we want and eliminate stress from our lives.

The first step in establishing your FitPlan is realizing how much money you or your household has coming in every month. From this point, you should take at least 10–15 percent off the top and make sure it is going to a savings account, which could be a bank account, investment account, or retirement account. Your income, less this number, should be your starting point. For example, if you make $2,000 a month (before taxes), then $200–300 a month should be going into a savings vehicle. So your true starting point would be $1,700–$1,800 a month. (Most planners, myself included, encourage people to take the 10–15 percent number from the gross salary—before taxes—and not the net salary—after taxes. I know that your paycheck will be less after the government gets its fair share, but you should think about paying yourself first and strive for saving that larger amount each year.)

Then subtract your taxes and "needs" categories: rent, car payment, student loan payment, and so forth. Do you have any money left? If you do not have any money left after saving, taxes, and needs, then you need to truly reflect on your lifestyle. Remember what I said earlier, "You Can't Always Get What You Want"? If you cannot afford a car or rent based on your salary, then you have to make difficult choices. Can you live in a cheaper part of town? Can you live at home?[1] Can you live with a roommate? Do you need to find a new job? Can you take mass transportation?

You would be surprised at the number of people I sit with who have no money left after subtracting out their needs. This typically happens because the client has access to credit cards or money from relatives. The issue with having access to credit cards is that it falsely leads you to think that you have money that you do not. If you are not earning the money as income, then you don't have it. The issue I have with support from relatives is that it prevents my clients from truly understanding how to live a life based on their income. I live and work in New York, and I advise a number of clients who live there also. It is an incredibly expensive place to live; however, I have seen many clients who are capable of living, working, and saving in New York, even on relatively small salaries. It requires hard work and focus, but they accomplish it by practicing many of the exercises in this book.

Once you have subtracted the needs, what you have left allows

---

1   Please note that just because I suggest living at home with relatives does not mean that I think you should live for free or create financial stress for your family. When I advise clients to live at home, I suggest that they pay rent to their relatives at a fair rate that may still be less than rent for an apartment. If the family needs the income, then they should use the rent money; however, if the family does not need the additional income, then it should be put into a savings account for the client to help him or her build the cash bucket.

for your wants. The great thing about starting a plan this way is that the first thing you did was put money aside for saving, so if you have money left over after savings, taxes, and needs, then you can truly feel good about "indulging" in wants. I encourage clients to list wants as specifically as possible, e.g., "food money," "going out money," "clothes money," and so forth. If you have money left over for this category, you want to make sure that you understand what you have earmarked that money for. The more specific you can get, the more freedom and understanding you will have with your spending.

Many people plan or budget for their needs and then lump their wants in a separate category. When you give each want category a specific definition, it helps you manage it better every month and determine whether your plan is a good one or whether it needs tweaking. For example, you may give yourself $100 a month for going out. If you are three weeks into the month and you have already spent the $100, then you know that you will spend the next week at home. Or you may look at your other wants categories (e.g., clothes, shoes) and see that you did not spend as much over the month in those areas and decide if you want to spend that on going out for the remainder of the month.

If you have anything remaining after saving, needs, and wants, then you have flexibility to do a number of things. As you can imagine, I advise my clients to add anything left over to savings or to apply that amount to their various debts. In fact, if there were a debt management issue, I would prioritize that within the client's needs and wants according to the situation. Remember: The most important goal of this exercise is to make sure that saving comes first. Once we build up the savings account, then we can determine how and where we need to deploy it, and that could be paying down debts or building assets.

The funds left over after savings, needs, and wants are the fuel that can be added to help you get ahead in your journey. That said, I do have some clients who have these excess funds and plan for waste money. They need to know that they can have some funds dedicated to those times when they want to splurge and not feel bad about it. Just as I advise you to be specific with your needs and wants, you should be specific with your wastes or excess income. Many of my clients will actually create savings accounts specifically for these items and name the savings accordingly: "Travel Money" or "Shopping Money." Again, it helps to know that you have money specifically set aside for paying down credit cards or buying apps, purses, and so forth.

The process of creating the FitPlan actually gives you tremendous freedom in your financial life. And I am sure you think I am crazy, as I am describing as "freeing" scenarios that seem limiting, but I have found that this sort of structure truly provides this feeling to my clients. When they understand that they *can* or *cannot* spend their money on certain things or experiences, it actually gives them a sense of peace. Before they had fitness plans in place, they spent money haphazardly and frequently wondered if they had the money or not. Or they would "worry about it later." After putting a plan in place, despite the initial fear of the plan constricting their life, they realize that it actually does the opposite.

Below I share an example of a typical plan that I encourage my clients to put together. Here are the steps to create it:

1. Determine your spending categories based on your fine-tooth comb exercise.

2. Take 10–15 percent of your gross income and put this number into your savings category first.

3. Fill in your needs costs per month.

4. Based on what is available for your wants, fill in these amounts per month.

5. If you have funds left over after needs and wants, determine what category you would like to add money to. In my worksheet this would be the "difference" category (e.g., Travel, Fun Money, etc.)

I encourage you to make your plan specific to you and to what is important to you. The more you own it, the more closely you will be able to follow it. Again, it may seem tedious and limiting, but I assure you that after a few months of living on a plan, you will think differently.

ENVELOPE SYSTEM

A number of my clients have a difficult time understanding how much money they are spending because they typically use credit cards more than they should. Or they will go through the process of creating their FitPlan but have a difficult time tracking it because they are using credit and debit cards and do not always update their monitoring system. A great solution for these issues is creating envelopes for the funds that you allocated through your FitPlan. If you designated $200 a month for food, then you should take out $200 once a month and put this in your food envelope and only use the funds from this envelope to pay for food. If you are getting close to the end of the month and there is not much cash in the envelope, then you will know that you have to eat what you have on hand or make different plans. I would encourage you to create an envelope for as many categories on your FitPlan as possible. Then you should also create a "fun" envelope. You can use this envelope to hold the funds that remain in the other envelopes at the end of the month. This is your reward for responsible planning during the month.

	Monthly Budget	Yearly Budget
Income		
Income		
Investment Income		
Budget Income Total		
Expenses		
Auto		
Bank Charges		
Charity		
Dining Out		
Education		
Entertainment		
Gifts (Birthdays, Holidays)		
Groceries		
Home		
Insurance		
Medical		
Miscellaneous		
Personal Care		
Pets		
Phone		
Recreation		
Retail		
Savings		
Taxes		
Travel		
Utilities		
Expense Total		
Difference (Income–Expense)		

COMMIT TO YOUR PLAN

It takes time and energy to come up with a FitPlan, and you may think it is a waste. But it is only a waste if you are never going to follow it or revise it. After you create this plan, you need to determine how you will be best able to follow it. I provide software and trainers for my clients to keep them on track; there are some great planning tools and apps—such as Mint.com and MoneyWiz—that can help keep you on track for achieving your goals. If this is the first time you are putting a plan together and attempting to live by it, please understand that this is a *difficult* process and results will not be achieved overnight. You will stumble and make mistakes. However, you cannot let that knock you off track or bring you down.

When I was going through Weight Watchers, I would have days when I ate or drank more than I was allowed and wished that I could just quit the program. However, I took those days in stride and continued with the program. If I had given in, I never would have achieved my goal. If you find that you are failing frequently, then stop yourself and review your plan. Maybe it is unrealistic in some areas. You may need to ask for help. Tell friends that you need to stop doing something and have them check you on your behaviors.

The plan is the best way to keep you on track for achieving your financial goals, but you have to make it a priority and live it. You need to understand that this plan is a living, breathing reality. Its purpose is to help give you a guideline for your year, but it can change. Life is unpredictable, and when we have changes, we need to adjust for them. I sit down with my clients every year, and we review and adapt their FitPlans. We reflect on how successful they were in following the previous year's plan and where they want to do things differently in the next year. We take into account their near- and long-term goals and where they are in their journey, and we incorporate all of this into their plan.

I AM NOW FINANCIALLY FIT!

Just as the process of getting physically fit is not an overnight one, the process of getting Financially Fit also requires commitment and patience. That said, based on your level of commitment to your plan, you will find that over the course of six months to a year, you will see tremendous results, and you will feel as though you are Financially Fit. By now, you have been focused on living a financially healthier lifestyle. After focusing on the details, targeting problem areas, and committing to a financial fitness plan, you are starting to see results: smaller credit card balances or lower debts and increased bank account balances. When you get to this place and feel that you have truly changed your past behaviors, then I think it is safe to say that you can call yourself Financially Fit. However, just because you are Financially Fit does not mean the process stops.

Just as with weight loss and staying physically fit, financial fitness is an ongoing effort that takes constant work and vigilance. As I mentioned in the introduction, certain sections like the one below will seem repetitive; however, I have tailored this section to someone who was previously Financially Skinny. I share this because even though you have achieved your financial goals, you have the potential to slip back into your past behaviors. Just as some people need to work harder at keeping weight off than others, Financially Skinny and Financially Fat people will have to work harder than intrinsically Financially Fit people until they have been practicing financial fitness long enough that it becomes part of their nature to consistently make financially fit choices. This is not a good or a bad thing; it is just a fact and something you should always keep in the back of your mind. Now that you are actively practicing Financially Fit habits, there are other areas of your financial life that can be put into focus.

USING CREDIT

As a Financially Skinny person, you are likely not a stranger to credit. Through the process of becoming Financially Fit, you may have even grown to detest your credit cards as you realized that they created more problems for you and made it difficult to achieve your financial goals.

When credit is not used wisely, it is absolutely a bad thing and you should detest it; however, there are many techniques and strategies for making credit a positive influence in your life. Hopefully, you have cleaned yours up if it was a problem and have not lost the ability to gain access to credit. Let's explore some smart strategies and benefits for utilizing credit.

INTEREST EARNED ON YOUR MONEY

Typically when you purchase something with credit, you have at least thirty days until you have to pay the credit card company. Take for example a $1,000 purchase. If you were going to pay cash for this item, the cash would come out of your checking account immediately. If you utilized a credit card, though, you would have an additional thirty days of this cash sitting in your bank account.

If your bank paid you 5 percent on your cash, and if you had $1,000 in the bank, this would amount to a little over $4 for the month. You may think that sounds like a small amount of money, but I bet if you found $4 on the street you would be excited about it. Why not find it in your own bank account? I always tell clients that interest paid to you by banks is "free money."

The relatively small size of the interest earned does not change the fact that it is free, and you should value it as such. If you are looking at a purchase of this size or larger from a store that offers free financing for a period of time, then the same rule applies. Plus, you get even more time to earn free money. If you were going to spend the same $1,000 and got "free financing" for twelve months, then this would mean that you had twelve months for your money to earn interest for you. At 5 percent, you are now looking at $50 for the year. Imagine if you found $50 on the street!

These strategies obviously only work if you plan to pay the credit card company back before interest and penalties are charged. My clients make sure that they give themselves reminders with plenty of time before the due date so that they do not incur undue penalties. And remember, anything that you purchase with credit should be part of your FitPlan at this point.

POINTS/REWARDS AND CASH BACK

Many companies offer cards that give you points, rewards, or cash back on money that you spend with the card. This is another way that you can get free money, this time from the credit card company. Depending on the card, on average, you can expect to get 1 percent back on what you spend or 1 percent toward points or rewards.

Going back to the $1,000 purchase, this would mean for every $1,000 you spend, you would get a $10 value in either cash or rewards. If you were already planning on spending this money, then why not get rewarded for doing so?

There are many types of rewards cards, and I always advise clients to utilize the ones that would provide the most meaningful rewards. I have a client who only flies Southwest Airlines and likes to travel. So she utilizes the Southwest credit card, and her spending helps pay for her trips. Because she is earning points on money she was going to spend anyway, we can put it to work elsewhere at the same time. I have some clients who like to give money to charity, and there are a number of cards that will let you do just that.

I know a number of people who also take advantage of the signup bonus on rewards cards, where if you spend a certain amount of money on the card in a given period, you will be given extra rewards and points. This is a great strategy to utilize when you know you have a large impending purchase.

The only catch with rewards cards is the possibility of an annual fee, which is how many of these card companies fund their rewards programs. Depending on the rewards level, the fee may be reasonable. If your annual fee were $100, then you would be paying around $8 a month for the benefit of using this card. As long as your rewards are more than $8 a month, then the fee makes sense. So, if you spend $1,000 a month and get $10 back, $8 would go to the fee and $2 would be your truly free money.

If you cannot easily determine the annual fee on the rewards card, call the company and ask. Look for rewards cards with no annual fee as well, or for card companies that will give you the first year free.

IMPROVED CREDIT SCORE

As a Financially Skinny person you may or may not have good credit. It is important to grasp that using credit wisely actually improves your credit score. If you used credit poorly in the past, showing a change in behavior will look good for your credit score going forward. One of the strangest pieces of advice credit counseling companies give people with bad credit histories is to get more credit. What they are telling people is that they should show that they have changed and prove that they can use credit responsibly. Over a period of time, you will see improvements in your credit score. If you had good credit already, then you can continue to show improvement.

FLEXIBILITY IN CASE OF EMERGENCY

When you use credit, you free up your cash for other purposes, especially emergencies. Nowadays almost all merchants take credit cards for payment; however, these cannot always be used for everything. At the end of the day, cash is king, and it will remain so unless we have some global financial meltdown that requires us to start trading in gold, goods, and services again. Until that day, it is always wise to keep a responsible reserve of cash for emergencies.

It is important to note that when I mention using credit, I don't always mean credit cards. Let's look at the example of my wonderful friend who purchased his house with cash. He saved and worked hard for years to build up enough money to pay for his house and closing costs. The only problem with this strategy is that after he closed, he realized that his home needed some substantial repairs, and he did not have enough cash left in his reserves to pay for them. He ultimately was able to obtain a home equity line on his home to cover these repairs. The good news for him is that, as with a mortgage, he is able to deduct the interest he pays on his home equity line of credit from his tax return. The bad news is that he has less overall credit available (home equity lines are typically smaller than mortgages), and he has the possibility of paying more interest over time, depending on the type of home equity line he utilized.

As I frequently tell clients, their financial journey is a long one, and despite all of the planning you can do, you never know what unexpected situations can arise. Like a spare tire, a cash reserve is the best way to plan for those unexpected events on your life's journey. The optimal size of your cash reserve depends on many factors. When I have clients who intend to buy a home, we plan on a cash reserve for their down payment and closing costs, but I always make sure that they have four to six months of mortgage payments reserved and another reserve for repairs, especially if they are buying an older home. No matter how great your home inspector is or how reliable you think the previous owners are, you never know what issues may be lurking in your "used" home.

A bank or mortgage provider requires you to have enough cash for the down payment and closing costs, but they do not demand that you have cash beyond those figures (they primarily look at your income as an indicator of repayment after closing). Remember, a bank or mortgage company is just a pit stop on your journey through life, and they are not really concerned with you beyond that one initial stop. I want to see you have the ability to make *all* of the stops you would like to make.

There are many opinions on how to manage the types of credit that you have, and I encourage you to constantly compare what interest rates you are paying across these types of credit options. I sometimes see clients with balances on credit cards with interest rates of 15–20 percent; however, they have or could have a home equity line of credit that they could utilize to pay down the credit cards and pay less than 6 percent. On $10,000, this could save you $900 a year. Using credit like mortgages, credit cards, or home equity lines may cause you some interest payments that you did not want to make. However, they give you more freedom with your cash, which could be worth more than that down the road.

USE YOUR CREDIT CARD MORE

Whether you had a problem in the past or you have managed your credit well, I challenge you to start using it more. Think about the times when you use your debit card or pay with a check and determine whether you can change your payment method to a credit card. For every time that you use the card, keep your receipt and do not pay the card right away. Wait until your credit card payment date and then pay the bill. If you make a practice of this strategy and it becomes part of your routine, you will earn more money in your checking or savings accounts, and you can earn points and rewards, depending on your card type.

INVESTING WISELY

Now that you have been saving more money, focusing on your investments should become more of a priority. Many people who have not had money to invest before are unsure what to do or may not want to take any risks, as they have worked so hard to even have money to invest.

I have mentioned before that I became disillusioned with the attempt to predict the performance of financial markets while I worked at the wealth management firm, but I still find value in them. I believe that over time, and with a well-diversified portfolio that is rebalanced at least once a year, you can achieve 6–8 percent returns. There are risks to achieving this performance; however, I feel that it is a good and achievable estimate.

Those of us who had money invested in stocks from 2000 to 2012 find it difficult to believe that there is much value in the financial markets. And when you look at stocks over this period of time, this assessment is pretty much true. The stock market was basically flat during this time, meaning that if you invested $100 in 2000, you would have $100 in 2012. Some people reading this may even have lost money in the markets at this time. There were a number of significant drops in stocks, but there were also significant gains. The issue with performance in people's investment portfolios over this period of time was not the fact that they were invested in stocks; it is that they were invested in *too much* stock and not in enough other investments.

While stocks did not perform well in recent years, the bond market did. If you have a well-diversified portfolio, meaning you invested in stocks *and* bonds, then you had better returns than someone who did not.

When you make any investment with your money, there are always risks; however, it is important to understand the types of money you have and what is appropriate for each money type. I always tell my clients that they have three buckets of money: cash, "moon" money, and "life" money.

Cash is the money that you might need for living expenses within the next six months to a year (depending on how conservative you are) should any catastrophic life event happen, such as a job loss or death of a spouse. Cash should typically be kept in a bank, savings account, or money market mutual fund—i.e., very conservative investments that are available to you daily. You want to take minimal risk with this money, as it represents your emergency funds.

Moon money represents the funds that you will need to draw during retirement. I call it moon money because if you are under 59½ years old or more than ten years from retirement, this is money that you should not touch. When you think of accessing it, consider it as easy to reach as the moon. Moon money should be invested the most aggressively. You have time until your retirement, so these funds can fluctuate up and down with the markets. Over time, they will make you more money than your bank account, despite the fact that sometimes it does not feel like it.

That leaves us with life money. This is the money that you have saved that allows you to live the life you want by doing things like buying a home or going on vacation. This money gives you the most flexibility to live your life. And many clients, especially Fit people, believe that this money should be treated as cash and exposed to no risk whatsoever. I understand this thought process. This is the money that is reserved for "life," and no one wants his or her life to be at risk. However, if you do not plan to utilize this money in the next two to five years, then it should not be sitting in a checking account. It should not be invested as aggressively as the moon money, but it should be invested in something more aggressive than a bank account. As the time comes closer to using the money, it should be moved into the cash bucket. Until then, it should be working for you by earning interest or growing in value.

I had clients who kept a significant amount of money (greater than $50,000) in a checking account. They only needed a small portion of this money for cash and emergencies; therefore, we invested the remainder into bond funds. These are more risky than a bank account and could lose value on any given day; however, over a period of two to five years, they will earn more money than in a bank account.

Depending on how long and how well you have been practicing good financial health, you may or may not have enough saved to have three buckets. You may just have enough for one, the cash bucket. But as you continue on your path and become more and more Financially Fit, you will have enough for three buckets. You should remember that each one should be progressively riskier. When you separate the three and invest wisely, your buckets will grow over time with minimal effort on your part.

BUCKETS

Reserve some time in your calendar to review your money and where you have it invested or deposited. Look at the total picture and determine whether you have three buckets (cash, life money, and moon or retirement money) or just one or two. If you have fewer than three, determine which bucket needs more. If you have three buckets, review what they are invested in. If they are too conservative, think about ways to take on more risk. You can speak to a financial adviser or consult with any number of financial websites like ETrade, Fidelity, Vanguard, or Charles Schwab.

INVESTMENTS

If you realized that your investments in your life or moon buckets are too conservative, you need to take some time to educate yourself on taking proper investment risk. Most of my clients who are not investing as much as they should are typically not doing it because they are afraid of the unknown. They have not had enough education on investing. I know that for some people, investing money seems incredibly scary and complicated—I was one of those people. However, with some education and practice, it really is not that scary. The first resource I tell clients to utilize is their own investment firm. If you already have a retirement account or brokerage account with ETrade, Fidelity, or any other firm, you should feel free to use their resources. After all, your balances are making them money, so you should feel free to benefit in return. Many of these websites have great online classes and tutorials, or you can always call their 800 numbers and speak to an adviser. If you choose to speak with an adviser, make sure that the adviser explains concepts to you until you understand them. I hate to see people invest in things and not fully understand them because they were afraid to ask questions. Ask lots of questions! It's your money, and you deserve to feel completely comfortable with what you do with it.

I also think there are a number of great blogs out there that explain investing in a very useful manner; you will discover many just by searching "finance blogs." I have recently started a YouTube channel where I discuss various investment topics, and I encourage you to check it out.

Just as it takes time to get physically fit, it takes time to gain an understanding of investments; however, it is time that is very well spent, in my opinion. I encourage you to dedicate time to finding the investment resources that most appeal to you, and spend some time each week reviewing them. Once you have gone through the exercise of determining your money buckets and how much should be put in each, it will be a matter of determining the best asset allocation for each bucket. When you are researching your investment options, look for those that will meet your asset allocation needs. Generally speaking, your cash bucket options should have a conservative asset allocation, your life bucket options should be moderately conservative to moderate, and your moon bucket options should be moderately aggressive to aggressive. Knowing your appropriate asset allocation actually makes the selection of investments a much easier process. And again, many of the financial websites provide guidance on what asset allocation might be best for you, based on your life goals.

CHAPTER 5

Financially Fat

OMG! I'm fat? I hate to be the one to break it to you, but yes, you are Financially Fat. When I told people what I was going to name the third category, I frequently got the response, "Isn't that harsh?" or "Doesn't that sound too negative?" or "Won't that turn people away?" The answer to all of those questions was "possibly" . . . but that does not detract from the truth of the description, and I believe in being honest with myself and with my clients. Just as people who have an overeating problem are fat, so are people who have an overspending problem. Financially Fat people have a habit of spending significantly more than they are saving and frequently spend more than they actually make, no matter how much they make. Many people think that someone who earns a high salary would be automatically Financially Fit; however, I have seen many high earners fall into the Financially Fat category. A Financially Fat person typically carries credit card balances that they cannot pay off each month, and their savings accounts are either non-existent or would not cover their lifestyle for more than a month or two should they lose their job.

There was a period in my life when I was both physically and Financially Fat. Despite the fact that my scale and my credit cards were telling me the truth, I refused to see it. I told myself that I was fine and that I was like other people, so my financial choices were not a problem. Therefore, I never made changes in my financial life.

In 2011, I finally accepted the fact that I was physically fat and decided to make a commitment to Weight Watchers. When I started the program, I was 5'5", I weighed 205 pounds, and I was a size fourteen (I probably could have fit into a sixteen, but refused to make that leap and just bought Spanx instead). Below is a picture of the physically fat me.

I began the road to weight loss in August of that year, and it wasn't until December that I felt as though I was starting to make a noticeable difference in my appearance. And it wasn't until May that I achieved my goal weight of 150 pounds. Yes, I did it! I *never* thought I would be able to do it, and it clearly was not an overnight process; however, it was an achievable goal. Once I had my physical house in order, so to speak, I felt ready to tackle my finances. It's funny, because it was easier for me to see the plan to get physically fit than to see the plan for financial fitness. They are very similar, though, and I apply this process to my clients who are Financially Fat.

So, yes, it does not sound good to be fat, and it does not feel good to be fat. You are probably constantly stressed about your spending, and yet you can't stop yourself. And when you are stressed about your spending, the one thing that you feel can make you happy is probably more spending—which only stresses you out more. It's okay. The fact that you are reading this book is a great first step, and I guarantee that if you follow the steps and the exercises, you can stop being Financially Fat. You can do it! Let's get started learning how!

ADMIT THAT YOU HAVE A PROBLEM

This first step may seem silly and pointless, but it is actually the most important step on your road to financial fitness. Out of the three financial types, you are the least "healthy," which means you have more financial habits or practices that need to be adjusted. You have a lot of work ahead of you, and if you do not believe you have a problem, then you will not be as committed to being part of the solution. I was Financially Fat for thirteen years but did not think that I had a problem. As I have found with many people who make money, I thought that I would just make more and that would cure my problems. This is a great plan as long as you are making money. However, if the revenue dries up or you decide you would like to pursue other hopes and dreams that are not as financially lucrative, you have a problem. Many physically skinny young people have similar behaviors. They eat and do whatever they want because they have a high metabolism and "just can't gain weight." Then they get older and their metabolism slows down. Unfortunately, they have never had to watch what they eat, so they don't know how to eat better or work out more. Then they begin to gain weight.

When you admit that you have a problem with your finances, then you are committing to working through the issues. Don't be afraid to admit you have a problem. Believe me, you are not alone. I have found that more people than not have problems with their personal finances. As I have said before, no one has to stay Financially Fat. You can correct this situation, and the realization and acceptance of being Financially Fat is a critical first step.

ACKNOWLEDGING THAT YOU ARE FINANCIALLY FAT

Most people who are Financially Fat suspect they have a problem because they know that they spend as much or more than they earn or their consumer debt keeps them awake at night. Perhaps you did not know you were Financially Fat until you took my quiz. Either way, take a few minutes to think about your financial life to date. What do you think led you to become Financially Fat? Are you an overspender? Do you use credit cards too often? Do you have emotional triggers where money is concerned? Do you spend too much time shopping? Do you go out too much? Come up with a list of five reasons why you are Financially Fat. Write them down. Keep this list to refer back to as you go through this process. I am a big proponent of letting things go and moving forward. This list is the beginning of you letting go of your past life of financial fatness and moving forward into financial fitness.

REALIZE THAT THIS IS NOT AN OVERNIGHT FIX

As I mentioned at the beginning of this chapter, I used to be fifty pounds overweight. I gained most of this weight over the course of three years. Every so often, I would get tired of being overweight and try to lose weight. I tried cleanses, pills, and extreme workouts. I would commit to these efforts for a few weeks at a time, achieve varying degrees of success, and then stop them. I typically stopped because I was not seeing dramatic results as rapidly as I wanted. In some cases, I even gained weight through the process. We are an instant gratification society and we want results as soon as possible. In many areas of our life, this is a very realistic expectation. I learned, though, that this is not a realistic expectation when it comes to lifelong weight loss. The same reality applies for lifelong financial fitness. I lost a little over one pound a week on Weight Watchers. When I originally started, I was incredibly frustrated by the snail's pace at which I was moving. However, I was committed to the process. I knew I was finally ready to make the change, and I taught myself patience.

If you are Financially Fat, your road to financial fitness will not be a short, easy one. You have spent years making yourself Financially Fat, and you cannot change these patterns and behaviors in a matter of days. But do not let this get you down. Just because your road will be long does not mean that it can't be fun and it won't be fruitful. I have been working with clients for over a decade, and I have always found that I have the best and most successful relationships when I manage my clients' expectations. If a process is going to be tedious or an investment volatile, I share this with my clients, and then when this expectation becomes a reality, I have a contented client rather than a frustrated one, because they were prepared for the event to occur.

I bring this up because I want to manage your expectations as you go through this process. If you have a large amount of debt, you cannot expect that it will go away in a few weeks. Or if you finally get to the point where you are saving, you cannot expect to have thousands of dollars in your bank account immediately. But if you commit to the process, do your exercises, and stick with the plans, over time you will have lower debt and higher savings. I can absolutely guarantee you that!

PATIENCE

Visualize what financial fitness looks like to you. Is it lower credit? Is it more savings? Is it financial freedom (i.e., the ability to do what you want when you want)? Create a distinct image of what this looks like. If you have words for it, then write them down. If you have images, then save them to your phone or a Pinterest page or print them out. There will be times when you feel like you are not achieving your success as rapidly as you would like, and when you feel like that, refer to these words or images. Keep them as your motivation. This is akin to "keeping your eyes on the prize." It always helps to have a written or visual representation of what the prize is, and this will be yours.

TAKE THINGS ONE STEP AND ONE DAY AT A TIME

Okay, so by this point in the process, we have acknowledged that we have a problem, and we realize that there is not an overnight fix. We are now ready to get on the road to financial fitness. The next thing we need to focus on is trying to help ourselves in small doses, one day at a time. As I mentioned earlier in the book, your financial life is like a cross-country road trip, where we will all end up in California, AKA retirement. This journey is similar to a physical fitness regimen in which the state of your body determines how long your process will take. This is similar to the state of your financial health. A Financially Fit person will start the journey in New York in a fuel-efficient or hybrid vehicle, while a Financially Skinny person will be traveling on a moped starting from Massachusetts, and a Financially Fat person will start out in

Maine, or maybe even Canada, traveling in a rundown, gas-guzzling clunker (the type of car the US government want off the roads).

You may say, "Shannon, what's wrong with Canada or a clunker?" You may love your clunker because you are comfortable in this car; however, it is also the least practical. And Canada is a lovely country, but starting in Canada puts you days or possibly weeks behind your Financially Fit friends, and in a long journey, every day counts. In addition, every dollar counts, and that clunker will consume much more in gas and maintenance than the hybrid. It will also make it difficult for you to make stops and see things that you want to see, because it may be apt to break down and need repairs.

You may be starting in the clunker in Canada, but one day at a time, you will make progress toward your goal and eventually you will get into your own hybrid and make up for lost time. You will have days when it is harder to stay on the path to financial fitness; however, I encourage you to remember that each day is important. If you have a setback, do not give up. Realize that it is just one day of many and continue on the path. This section will help you manage your expectations. When you understand that this is a long road, then you can navigate the smaller bumps along the way. It will be important to make goals that are reasonable and break them down into segments. Again, a 3,000-mile road trip is a lot to think about trying to do in one day; however, if you think about breaking it up into a few miles a day, it is not so bad.

DIAGNOSE YOUR MAJOR AREAS OF CONCERN

I hope I have managed your expectations about the journey to becoming Financially Fit, so let's now start tackling our situation head on. For you, as a Financially Fat person, after admitting the problem and realizing you have a long road ahead, the next step is discovering your major problem areas. If you go back to the first exercise of this chapter, you may have uncovered these. If you are not aware of your problem areas off the top of your head, then pull up your credit card or bank statements and look for charges that stick out to you.

Do you have too many charges in clothing stores? Do you pay a lot in rent or mortgage? Do you eat out a lot? Do you just plain use your credit card too much? For most Financially Fat people, major areas of concern should be easy to spot. They are the ones where you have spent the majority of your money over a period of time. I had a major problem with eating out. Other than my mortgage or rent payment, it was the next highest expense category in my monthly budget.

If you did not uncover these areas in the first exercise, take the time to try to figure out how you got here. When I was physically fat, I knew it was because I ate and drank too much—these were my major problem areas. Create a list of your problem areas, being as specific as possible, e.g., "Mortgage" or "J Crew" or "Bars" or "Shoes." Writing the list will help you see what your enemy is. This list is your kryptonite, your biggest hurdle to achieving financial fitness. This will be one of the most important tasks you do as you move forward. Identifying the problem is mission-critical; otherwise, how are you going to know how to address it?

If you are having a difficult time identifying your problem areas, ask your friends or family. You will be amazed at how well they can point out your flaws for you. When I started losing weight, I had a number of people say to me, "Yeah, I thought you ate out too much." Really? I wondered. Why didn't they tell me that before? The response they would give me was, "You never asked." If you ask, I am sure you will get answers. And a word of caution: You will more than likely not be pleased with the response you get from your loved ones, but you need to keep things in perspective. Remember, at the beginning of this, you recognized that you had a problem. Now we are all working toward a solution, and honesty from your friends and family will get you there faster.

CREATE FUN STRATEGIES FOR FIXING YOUR PROBLEM AREAS

Once you have identified your major problem areas, you need to strategize the best way to neutralize them. Everyone is different, and what works for some people may not work for others. Therefore, you need to think about the best and most fun way you can shrink your problem areas. When I did this exercise with one client, we realized that her problem area was the rent that she was paying for her apartment. She was new to New York and wanted to live in a "nice" area that was convenient to her work and friends, but she did not want to have a roommate. As you can imagine, this left her with an apartment that cost well above the amount that she should have been paying, given her lifestyle and salary. Over time, this apartment led her to run up her credit cards, as she did not typically have much of her salary left to spend on her other needs and wants after paying rent.

We had a very long strategy session about the apartment and determined that she would either find a roommate or look in a different part of the city for a place to live. She ended up moving to Brooklyn and finding a bigger space than her Manhattan apartment, and she grew to love her new neighborhood. The best result of this exercise, though, was the fact that she saved over 20 percent a month and caught up on her bills.

I have another client who had a shopping problem. When we discussed problem areas, she did not even need to look at her credit card statement to know what she needed to work on. She likened her shopping habit to a drug addiction that she didn't know how to kick. For her, we utilized the visualization strategy to help her tackle this problem. She wanted to travel more but did not have the resources after her shopping expenditures. So she saved a picture on her phone of a resort that she wanted to go to. Whenever she would go into a store, she would pull up the picture of the beach and know that a purchase would keep her from getting there. After a few months of this, she got to the point where she didn't even want to go shopping as much as she used to, or if she went, she was able to control her spending without having to look at the picture.

One of my clients had a problem with going out too much, a common problem for many people in NYC or any major city. The convenient location of bars and restaurants makes it very easy to spend lots of time in them. In addition, the fact that just about every bar accepts credit cards makes it easier to spend money. And my client would not only spend money on himself, but also on other people. After all, when your card is with the bartender, it is very easy to add drinks to your tab. Then the more you drink, the better you feel and the more you forget what is on your tab. He would typically end the night signing his receipt but having no clue what he spent; he could barely read, due to the large quantities of alcohol he had consumed. He usually did not know the damage until the next day, when he would log into his bank account online. For him, it was difficult to stay home and say no to friends. He was young, he worked hard, and he wanted to play hard.

To help this client, we needed to find replacement activities and behaviors so that he did not feel "deprived." He committed to spending a few evenings a week at home, but he did this with his group of friends, and they rotated whose apartment they would hang out in each night. The host would buy pizza, and the friends would each bring a six-pack.

They ended up playing cards and/or watching a sporting event or movie on TV. Over a period of two months, this group realized that among the five of them, they saved over $1,000 by staying in versus going out. This same client also challenged himself to go out with cash instead of credit cards. I frequently challenge my clients to do this very thing. Set aside a certain amount of cash you can spend responsibly in one night, and have only that amount and your ID on you. When your money runs out, you know that it is time to go home or to find people to buy your drinks for you. If your evenings end earlier than you would like, then find different places to drink or establishments that offer drink specials. I have never had a client fail at this challenge, and most of them have fun trying to succeed.

PROBLEM MINIMIZATION

Now that I have given you a few examples, I challenge you to brainstorm ways that you can minimize your problem areas. Do you need to remove the problem completely, as in the case of the apartment? Will visualization help you? Is there something equally fun—just different and less expensive—that you can replace this with? As you implement this plan, start tracking how much you save by having the strategy in place (e.g., if you go into a store, figure out how much you would have spent if you weren't combating your shopping habit).

Saved money will not be obvious in your checking account; however, if you keep your own tally, you will see a growing number that should make you feel good about your efforts.

REWARD YOURSELF

I have a son, and he is a child who gave new meaning to the terms "terrible twos" and "trying threes." Those two years of his life seemed to be filled with a never-ending battle of the wills between him and us. We tried every method of punishment to change his behavior. Finally, we enlisted the help of a family coach who informed us that we should not, in fact, punish him, but rather reward him. She stated that children react better to positivity than negativity. This was a revelation to us. After all, this was not how we grew up. If my mother yelled at me, I listened and stopped doing whatever I was doing that got me into trouble. So, with the help of the coach, we created a rewards chart for my son, and rather than point out his flaws and make him feel bad about himself, we rewarded his appropriate activities. He could use the points that he earned with good behavior toward gifts of various sizes.

I use this same approach with my clients and encourage others to use it as well. After all, who does not like to receive a reward? As I have said multiple times, you are on a long road to financial fitness, and you need to reward yourself when you hit goals and milestones. As my son accomplished bigger and more difficult tasks, his rewards grew in size, and you should employ the same process. As you achieve bigger savings goals or credit reduction goals, give yourself a bigger reward.

YOUR REWARD CHART

Take the time out of your schedule to create a reward chart for yourself. Think about what your short- and long-term financial goals are and how you should reward yourself for achieving them. You can make this in Excel and add pictures or photos. If you are new to the financial fitness process, you can start with one or two easy goals, but as you do this for longer, you should challenge yourself to achieve more difficult goals. An example of a short-term goal is not using your credit card for a month, or spending only a certain amount of money a week, or paying down a certain amount of your student loans or credit cards. The goal should be achievable within a month, and at the end of the month, if you have accomplished the goal, give yourself a small reward. This could be an iTunes gift card, an extra cocktail when you go out, or a new pair of earrings.

An example of a long-term goal is something that you could accomplish within six months to a year. It could be the same as the short-term goal, only larger in size. If you accomplish this goal, you should have a bigger reward. This could be a new purse, a fancy dinner, or a nice bottle of wine. Please keep in mind that your rewards should not create additional financial burdens on you, so keep them appropriately sized, given your goals.

SURROUND YOURSELF WITH A SUPPORTIVE COMMUNITY

Financial fitness is something that does not come easily to most people, and as a Financially Fat person, it is not easy for you at all. You will have plenty of challenges and temptations along your path to financial fitness, so the last thing you need are friends and family who are not supportive of you. I attribute my success in weight loss to the fact that my husband did Weight Watchers with me. All of the other times when I would try to lose weight, he would eat or drink in front of me and create an easy temptation. Admitting that you have a financial problem is not easy, and for many people money is a very taboo subject; it is not something that friends or even family like to discuss with each other.

However, if you have a problem, you need to tell those around you and let them know that you are working to correct it. It is not something you should be ashamed of, and I think you will actually find many people in the same situation as you. They may be thankful that you are doing something about it and even join you.

A great example of this is the client I mentioned whose problem was going out too much. When he convinced his group of friends to spend evenings in, they were actually relieved that their wallets would get a break as well. No matter how much money we have or how much we make, it is always nice to save a little. If you find that you have friends or family who continue to tempt you with your spending weaknesses, then you need to think about taking some time away from them. If they are true friends, they will be there when you no longer find their lifestyles and activities tempting. If they are not, then maybe you have done yourself a favor in weeding them out.

WITH A LITTLE HELP FROM MY FRIENDS

Think about a friend or a group of friends that you hang out with frequently, and during an appropriate get-together, share with this group your struggles with your finances and how you plan to change this about yourself. Ask for their help or suggestions for ways you can save money and spend less. I have a client who is in a book club with a few women, and the book club decided to work together to brainstorm different ways they could all save money collectively. If you have a group of friends that meets once a week for cocktails, see if they are open to "nights in" where the goal is to spend the least amount of money but have the maximum amount of fun. Instead of shopping trips, try walking or hiking with a friend. I have another client who has made it a competition with her friend to see who can save the most (on a percentage basis) over a six-month period, and the loser has to buy dinner for the winner. See how many people you can enlist to join you on the road to financial fitness.

CONTINUOUSLY MONITOR YOURSELF

At this point, you have your eyes on your main problem areas, and you are working on them. Hopefully you will have many months of success, but I urge you to not become complacent or slip in any lasting way. If you have only been practicing Financially Fit behaviors for a few months, you have to remember that you had poor habits for much longer than that, and those poor habits have a way of creeping up when you least expect them. This is a common problem with people who have lost weight; they stop weighing themselves, and when they do, the pounds start to gradually creep back on. But if you constantly monitor yourself, then you can focus on losing the one to five pounds you may have gained. It is much easier to lose one to five than five to fifteen. The same is true for your finances. It is easier to nip things in the bud early on than when they have gotten too far out of control. You need to be constantly vigilant about what you are doing; otherwise, you will fall back into Financially Fat ways.

A good way to combat complacency is to schedule time with yourself and inventory your progress. Just as you would weigh yourself once a week for weight-loss progress, you should check in with yourself once a week as you are getting on this path. Once your path is well established, then you can check in once a month, then once a quarter. Put this time in your calendar and make it a formal process. Sit with your finances and track your results. Are you still on the path that you were hoping to be on? Have you slipped? If you have slipped, what can you do to get back on track?

SELF-MONITORING

During the first three months of financial fitness training, schedule a weekly meeting with yourself to look over your finances. After that, schedule a monthly meeting. Spend at least one hour of your time looking over your numbers. Examine your reward chart. Are you on target? Have you achieved your financial goals for the period? Are you doing the appropriate exercises? Have you had a setback? How can you correct this problem? Are your friends helping or hurting your progress?

I AM NOW FINANCIALLY SKINNY!

The primary goal of Financially Fat persons is to work on the big problem areas of their lives. Once they have those under control, then they can start to work on the fine details. Financially Skinny people have to work on the details. Think of this as having to lose fifty pounds. During your Financially Fat training, you were working on the first forty-five. Now you are moving into the Financially Skinny part of your financial journey, and you need to focus on the last five pounds. I tell clients that they are ready to focus on the "Skinny" work when they feel that they have a good hold on their bigger issues. There is no set timetable as to when this will happen for clients; it is different for everyone. However, the greatest indicator as to the speed of success is in the commitment that you put into the process. When my clients are really focused on achieving financial fitness success, they move through levels faster.

The steps that Financially Skinny people need to take to become Fit include:

1. pulling out the fine-tooth comb;
2. categorizing spending;
3. finding "minor" problem areas;
4. creating a "FitPlan";
5. committing to the plan.

PULL OUT THE FINE-TOOTH COMB

My Financially Skinny clients typically tell me that they "can't save money" and that they "live paycheck to paycheck." If you are not paying attention to the details, then those statements are absolutely correct. However, when I hear these claims, the first thing I tell them to do is open up their credit card and bank account statements. We typically review at least three to four months' worth of statements so that we can pick up any patterns or recurring items over that period of time.

From this point, we go through the statements with a fine-tooth comb. We evaluate and discuss *every single purchase*. This process may seem tedious and useless; however, you would be shocked at how many "little" items add up to something significant over time. I frequently have clients who have recurring charges on their cards that they didn't realize were there—I was one of those people myself. When I took out the fine-tooth comb, I realized that I was paying $9 a month for one credit-reporting agency and $14.95 for another to do the same thing. I was obsessed with my credit report for a while, convinced that someone was going to steal my credit information and ruin my score. Singularly, these charges did not mean much of a hardship for me. Combined, though, they represented almost $300 a year. Now, I love my credit score, but $300 could mean a lot more fun things—like shoes!

Other clients didn't realize how much their latté habit was costing them. Four dollars a day does not seem like much on its own. But over five days that is $20; over the course of a month, it is $80; and over the course of a year, it is $960. Do not think that I am bashing lattés or other small indulgences. I personally have a latté habit, and it is a daily ritual that I would not give up for anything in the world—so I have planned for it. But if you could drink coffee at work or at home instead, $960 is a great bonus you can give yourself fairly easily.

When you are Skinny, it is important to scrutinize every single purchase and spending habit that you have. One time I was going through this process with a client, and we realized that she was paying car insurance for a car she rarely drove. When we really analyzed the value of the insurance, we realized that it was an unnecessary expense that she could suspend until she used the car again. This decision added $1,200 to her bank account that year.

Sometimes we convince ourselves that our spending is necessary; however, when we take the time to truly question our spending, we start to realize that maybe some of the things we are doing are not so much necessary as just habits that we can live without.

If you have a difficult time questioning your spending habits, then I encourage you to invite a friend over and have him or her help you analyze the value of your purchases. Preferably this friend should be Financially Fit or Skinny, and not Fat, in order to be best equipped to help you analyze your spending objectively.

USING THE FINE-TOOTH COMB

Print out three to four months of credit and debit card statements. Yes, print them out! I find that people are able to analyze information better when it is in print. Then look at the expenses in order of size value and categorize them by high, medium, and low costs. Next, look at the frequency of each purchase. Do you see multiple charges for one location? Do you see daily or weekly charges for something? Is this a good thing or a bad thing? We will use this analysis in a later exercise.

CATEGORIZE YOUR SPENDING

In order to determine problem areas to target, you need to organize your spending into three categories: needs, wants, and wastes. A *need* is an expense that you truly cannot live without, and items in this category typically include rent or mortgage, insurance payments, and any other debt payments that you are obligated to make, like student loan debt and car payments. A *want* is something that you desire, but you can typically find a more cost-effective alternative. Examples of wants include food, gas, phone, and entertainment. And *wastes* are just as you would imagine; they do not typically create much value in your life, and purchasing them takes you further from your financial goals. Examples of wastes are clothes, shoes, apps, games, and so forth.

The three categories are important because many people often think that wants fall into their needs categories. Again, needs are really any fixed costs that you absolutely have to pay; after that, most items should fall into wants or wastes. I tell clients that food is a want because there are many ways that you can include food in your spending other than the way that you likely currently achieve it. Eating out every day, three meals a day is not the most cost-effective method for feeding yourself. If you are living paycheck to paycheck, then this is an easy area to start to fix right away. I used to fall into the trap of eating out too much; however, I was able to take control of my eating behaviors by planning my shopping better, and I cut my food costs by 70 percent, just by changing the way I ate.

I also have a number of clients who *love* eating organic food. I like organic food, but do you really need to eat certain types of food in organic form? When you truly analyze the value of organic, you will discover that it is not a necessity in certain areas. You are just falling prey to a very compelling marketing effort. An organic lifestyle is a want, not a need, in my mind. The fact is that organic foods could cost 50 to 100 percent more than their traditional counterparts. If you are spending $100 a week for food, you could potentially reduce that to $50 and save yourself $200 a month by lessening your organic consumption.

I don't want anyone to think that I am bashing organic food or the natural living industry. Rather, I mention organic food because I am concerned about your financial health, and I frequently see clients make themselves financially unhealthy in an effort to make themselves physically healthy. If you can afford to pay 50 to 100 percent more for organic food and you have planned for it, then I am supportive of that strategy. However, if you cannot afford to eat 100 percent organic, then do more research into the value of organic food. Or, limit yourself to those few items that are deemed necessary to avoid directly consuming pesticides and other harmful ingredients.

Another want often confused for a need is gas expenses for your car. Fuel prices are challenging for everyone who drives; however, sometimes driving (or at least driving alone) is not the only way that you can get where you need to go. I know that mass transit may not be appealing to you or may not be the most convenient method of transportation; however, if you could use it as an alternative to driving in certain circumstances, you could save yourself money on your gas costs. I also like to see clients try carpooling with their significant other or coworkers. Again, this may add some inconvenience or extra time to your schedule; however, in the process of achieving financial fitness, you will find that there are a number of "inconveniences" that will reap financial rewards for you down the road.

Just as wants can be confused with needs, many wastes are confused as well. I imagine that you have viewed many of these items as a need or a want. You will say, "Shannon, I *needed* to get a new phone." Or, "Shannon, I *needed* new clothes for work." You may *think* that you needed these things, and maybe you truly did. But could you have made better choices, instead of overspending and putting them in the waste category? I typically view wastes as purchases that set you further behind in achieving your financial goals. When you are looking at your waste items, a good rule of thumb is to ask yourself if the purchase helped or hurt you in reaching your financial goals. If it hurt you, then you know it belongs in the waste category. Later in the book, we are going to discuss putting your plan in place, and if you truly need some of these items and you plan for them, then it will not have been money wasted in your pursuit of financial fitness. However, if you did not plan for these items, then it is exactly the same as throwing your money in the garbage.

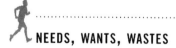

NEEDS, WANTS, WASTES

Review your spending from the last three to four months (you can use your information from the fine-tooth comb exercise) and try to place every dollar spent into one of these categories. If you have everything listed as a need, then you should go back and look at each item more objectively or ask for help in categorizing everything. Look at your wastes and add them up. How much could you have saved in three to four months if you had avoided wastes? Are there wants or wastes that can be eliminated or adjusted?

FIND YOUR "MINOR" PROBLEM AREAS

After going through the fine-tooth comb and "needs, wants, wastes" exercises, did you determine what I call "minor" problem areas? These represent continual spending behaviors that can be corrected. Minor problem areas are easy to find, because they will appear multiple times in your bank and credit card statements. A car payment or mortgage payment would not be a minor problem area, and not all minor problem areas can be completely resolved; however, the first step is acknowledging they exist so that you can determine whether there is a way to control them.

For example, when I started Weight Watchers, I knew that McDonald's was a minor problem area for me. Lacking self-control, I could not go there and order a salad or something that was low in Weight Watchers points. However, because I knew McDonald's was a minor problem area, I could create a plan to avoid it or manage it better. Similarly, I had a client who had a clothing store show up on her credit card statement more times than it should in any given month. Don't get me wrong—I love clothes shopping as much as the next person. However, this is not the type of store that should appear on your credit card statement more than a food store or gas station. We immediately knew this was a minor problem area for her and could deal with it accordingly.

Other problem areas that sometimes take work to consolidate include going out and recreation. One charge for Capital Grille does not seem like much, but when you have Capital Grille, Houston's, Applebee's, and PF Chang's and add them together, now it becomes a problem area. For young people in bigger cities, this typically happens with bars. I have a client who frequently does not know where she has been except by reviewing her debit card statement.

An often-concealed problem area is gas purchases. Most of us rarely go to the same station every time we fill up, so there could be multiple names that you have to identify and aggregate to determine whether this is a problem area for you to work on.

You may think all of this examination and consolidation is a waste of time, or you will tell me that there are budget programs like Mint .com that will point out these things for you. And it is true that some of these programs can consolidate information for you. However, none are perfect, and you will typically discover that you have a large category called "uncategorized" because the program does not know whether the location was a gas station or a restaurant. This "uncategorized" category prevents the eye-opening experience of truly seeing where your money goes. Most of my clients do not realize that they frequent places as much as they do or that they spend as much money as they do in certain areas.

Identifying problem areas is a huge step in achieving financial fitness. Sometimes we do not even realize that they are problems until we sit and analyze our spending. Once we know that they are keeping us from becoming Financially Fit, then we can find solutions to help us manage them so that they are less problematic.

TARGET AND ATTACK MINOR PROBLEM AREAS

If you have determined any minor problem areas above, write them down and strategize how to eliminate or work on them. Consider whether each is a problem because of the frequency of purchases, the size of purchases, or both. Do you need to go to Starbucks every day? Can you replace one of those Starbucks trips with coffee from home or a cart on the street? Are you going to J. Crew or any retail store too much? Determine why you are frequenting the store. Is it because it is on your way home? Can you plan a different way home? Can you walk into the store, find things you would want to buy, write down the prices, and simply walk out? If you are spending too much money on gas, is there another mode of transportation that you can take to save money? It is important to create specific plans for how you will overcome problem areas in your spending. Otherwise, they will continue to remain problems.

SPENDING——*STOP* AND *WHY*

Most people at various times in their life have spending problems. Some of us have it worse than others. I had a *very* bad spending problem, which stemmed from making good money and having credit. I always told myself there would be more money down the road, so I could put purchases on my credit card. I *never* thought there would be an end to the money. However, when I wanted to make a career change that would provide me less money but more fulfillment, I realized that I needed to control my spending. The basic tenets of financial health are earning more and spending less. If you cannot earn more, then you need to spend less. This exercise is the most valuable for helping my clients with their spending, and you can do it *every single day.* Every time that you are about to spend money, STOP yourself for a brief minute and ask WHY? Why are you buying what you are buying?

The great news for you is that there are only two correct answers to this question: (1) It is life and death. You will literally die if you don't buy health insurance or a medication or take a trip to the emergency room; (2) you have planned for it. If you made that purchase of the new phone or the clothes for work part of your plan for the year, then you can go ahead and buy that item. If one of these two answers was not applicable, put down that item, walk away, and don't look back.

THE FOLLOW-UP TO *STOP* AND *WHY*

So you have just practiced the STOP and WHY exercise, and you feel bad. You typically feel good buying things and spending money and you *really* wanted to spend the money you were just going to—but instead you practiced a financial fitness exercise, and now you feel bad. Now what? When you experience this level of sadness for not making a purchase, find a new outlet for the displaced happiness.

When I was losing weight, I really wanted to eat a cheeseburger. Eating a salad just didn't feel as good. So I would eat the salad and visualize the way it would make me look. Or I would let myself have the salad with a small treat like a glass of wine or a piece of candy. Similarly, the thing you were just about to buy was not part of your plan, but is there something else that is? Can you buy that instead?

You can also try distracting yourself with something that makes you happy. Call a friend, play an app on your phone, go for a walk. Try a number of different distracting exercises so that you do not fixate on the fact that you feel bad that you did not make that purchase. You do not want to feel as though you are deprived or missing out while you are on the road to financial fitness. If you do, then you are less likely to stay on this important path.

NO-SPEND DAYS

Another way to prevent yourself from having a spending issue is to commit to achieving a certain number of no-spend days a month. During a no-spend day, you literally will plan to not use your cash, debit, or credit cards for an entire day. It is a best practice to plan one of these a week, and an easy way to accomplish this exercise is just to take your driver's license out with you and leave the rest of your wallet home for the day. While you are practicing a no-spend day, make sure you reflect on where you would have spent money if you could have spent money. This is another great way for you to identify problem areas in your spending life.

CASH-ONLY DAYS

Similar to no-spend days, I think it is a best practice to have at least one cash-only day a week. The set amount of cash you allow yourself to spend during the day should be a difficult goal for you, and for most clients this number is usually around $20. Think of cash-only days like "push days" when you are working out at the gym. Maybe you can easily run two miles at a time, but on a push day, you make yourself run three. Maybe you normally spend $40 a day on various items, so push yourself once a week to only spend $20.

CREATE YOUR FITPLAN

At this point, you have gone through three to four months of spending with a fine-tooth comb, categorized your spending, and determined where your problem areas are. Now you need to determine what you are going to do about them. This is when we establish the fitness plan, or "FitPlan." The number one reason for my clients becoming Skinny or Fat is the lack of having a plan in place. Traditionally this plan is called a budget. Personally, I think that "budget" is another "four-letter word," like "diet." No one (except maybe a Fit person) likes the idea of living on a budget, so most choose not to. The truth is, we actually don't need a budget; we need a plan.

Going back to the road-trip analogy, doesn't it make more sense to plot out the trip on GPS or a map rather than get in a car and just drive? Without a FitPlan, this is exactly what we do every day in our financial lives, and then we wonder why we have overspent or live paycheck to paycheck. If we can plan for as much of our life as possible, then we are not limiting ourselves as we imagine we would be doing on a budget or diet. Instead, we are making a lifestyle change that will actually help us get what we want and eliminate stress from our lives.

The first step in establishing your FitPlan is realizing how much money you or your household has coming in every month. From this point, you should take at least 10–15 percent off the top and make sure it is going to a savings account, which could be a bank account, investment account, or retirement account. Your income, less this number, should be your starting point. For example, if you make $2,000 a month (before taxes), then $200–$300 a month should be going into a savings vehicle. So your true starting point would be $1,700–$1,800 a month. (Most planners, myself included, encourage people to take the 10–15 percent number from your gross salary—before taxes—and not your net salary—after taxes. I know that your paycheck will be less after the government gets its fair share, but you should think about paying yourself first and strive for saving that larger amount each year.)

Then subtract your taxes and needs categories: rent, car payment, student loan payment, and so forth. Do you have any money left? If you do not have any money left after saving, taxes, and needs, then you should truly reflect on your lifestyle. Remember what I said earlier, "You Can't Always Get What You Want"? If you cannot afford a car or rent based on your salary, then you have to make difficult choices. Can you live in a cheaper part of town? Can you live at home?[2] Can you live with a roommate? Do you need to find a new job? Can you take mass transportation?

You would be surprised by the number of people I sit with who have no money left after subtracting out their needs. This typically happens because the client has access to credit cards or money from relatives. The issue with having access to credit cards is that it falsely leads you to think that you have money that you do not. If you are not earning the money as income, then you don't have it. The issue I have with support from relatives is that it prevents my clients from truly understanding how to live a life based on their income. I live and work in New York and advise a number of clients who do the same. It is incredibly expensive to live in New York; however, I have seen many clients who are capable of living, working, and saving in New York, even on relatively small salaries. It requires hard work and focus, but they accomplish it by practicing many of the exercises in this book.

Once you have subtracted the needs, what you have left allows for your wants. The great thing about starting a plan this way is that

---

2   Please note that just because I suggest living at home with relatives does not mean that I think you should live for free or create financial stress for your family. When I advise clients to live at home, I suggest that they pay rent to their relatives at a fair rate that may be less than rent for an apartment. If the family needs the income, then they should use the rent money; however, if the family does not need the additional income, then it should be put into a savings account for the client to help him or her build the cash bucket.

the first thing you did was put money aside for saving, so if you have money left over after savings, taxes, and needs, then you can truly feel good about "indulging" in wants. I encourage clients to list wants as specifically as possible. e.g., "food money," "going out money," "clothes money," and so forth. If you have money left over for this category, you want to make sure that you understand what you have earmarked that money for. The more specific you can get, the more freedom and understanding you will have with your spending.

Many people plan or budget for their needs and then lump their wants in a separate category. When you give each want category a specific definition, it helps you manage it better every month and see if your plan is a good one or if it needs tweaking. For example, you may give yourself $100 a month for going out. If you are three weeks into the month and you have already spent the $100, then you know that you will spend the next week at home. Or you may look at your other wants categories (e.g., clothes, shoes) and see that you did not spend as much over the month in those areas, and decide you want to spend that money on going out for the remainder of the month.

If you have anything remaining after saving, needs, and wants, then you have flexibility to do a number of things. As you can imagine, I advise my clients to add anything left over to savings or to apply that amount to their various debts. In fact, if there were a debt management issue, I would prioritize that within your needs and wants according to your situation. Remember: The most important goal of this exercise is to make sure that saving comes first. Once we build up the savings account, then we can determine how and where we need to deploy it, and that could be paying down debts or building assets.

The funds left over after savings, needs, and wants are the fuel that can be added to help you get ahead in your journey. That said, I do have some clients who have these excess funds and plan for waste money. They need to know that they can have some funds dedicated to those times when they want to "splurge" and not feel bad about it. Just as I advise you to be specific with your needs and wants, you should be specific with your wastes or excess income. Many of my clients will actually create savings accounts specifically for these items and name the savings accordingly: "Travel Money" or "Shopping Money." Again, it helps to know that you have money specifically set aside for paying down credit cards or buying apps, purses, and so forth.

The process of creating the FitPlan actually gives you tremendous freedom in your financial life. And I am sure you think I am crazy as I am describing as "freeing" scenarios that seem limiting, but I have found that this sort of structure truly provides this feeling to my clients. When they understand that they *can* or *cannot* spend their money on certain things or experiences, it actually gives them a sense of peace. Before they had fitness plans in place, they spent money haphazardly and frequently wondered if they had the money or not. Or they would "worry about it later." After putting a plan in place, despite the initial fear of the plan constricting their life, they realize that it actually does the opposite.

Below I share an example of a typical plan that I encourage my clients to put together. Here are the steps to create it:

1. Determine your spending categories based on your fine-tooth comb exercise.

2. Take 10–15 percent of your gross income and put this number into your savings category first.

3. Fill in your needs costs per month.

4. Based on what is available for your wants, fill in these amounts per month.

5. If you have funds left over after needs and wants, determine what category you would like to add money to. In my worksheet this would be the "difference" category (e.g., Travel, Fun Money, etc.)

I encourage you to make your plan specific to you and what is important to you. The more you own it, the more closely you will be able to follow it. Again, it may seem tedious and limiting, but I assure you that after a few months of living on a plan, you will think differently.

ENVELOPE SYSTEM

A number of my clients have a difficult time understanding how much money they are spending, because they typically use credit cards more than they should. Or they will go through the process of creating their FitPlan, but have a difficult time tracking it because they are using credit and debit cards and do not always update their monitoring system. A great solution for these issues is creating envelopes for the funds that you allocated through your FitPlan. If you designated $200 a month for food, then you should take out $200 once a month and put this in your food envelope, and only use the funds from this envelope to pay for food. If you are getting close to the end of the month and there is not much cash in the envelope, then you will know that you have to eat what you have on hand or make different plans. I would encourage you to create an envelope for as many categories on your FitPlan as possible. Then you should also create a "fun" envelope. You can use this envelope to hold the funds that remain in the other envelopes at the end of the month. This is your reward for responsible planning during the month.

	Monthly Budget	Yearly Budget
Income		
Income		
Investment Income		
Budget Income Total		
Expenses		
Auto		
Bank Charges		
Charity		
Dining Out		
Education		
Entertainment		
Gifts (Birthdays, Holidays)		
Groceries		
Home		
Insurance		
Medical		
Miscellaneous		
Personal Care		
Pets		
Phone		
Recreation		
Retail		
Savings		
Taxes		
Travel		
Utilities		
Expense Total		
Difference (Income—Expense)		

COMMIT TO YOUR PLAN

It takes time and energy to come up with a FitPlan, and you may think it is a waste. But it is only a waste if you are never going to follow it or revise it. After you create this plan, you need to determine how you will be best able to follow it. I provide software and trainers for my clients to keep them on track; there are some great planning tools and apps such as Mint.com and MoneyWiz that can help keep you on track for achieving your goals. If this is the first time you are putting a plan together and attempting to live by it, please understand that this is a *difficult* process, and results will not be achieved overnight. You will stumble and make mistakes. However, you cannot let that knock you off track or bring you down.

When I was going through Weight Watchers, I would have days when I ate or drank more than I was allowed and wished that I could just quit the program. However, I took those days in stride and continued with the program. If I had given in, I never would have achieved my goal. If you find that you are failing frequently, then stop yourself and review your plan. Maybe it is unrealistic in some areas. Or ask for help. Tell friends that you need to stop doing something and have them check you on your behaviors.

The plan is the best way to keep you on track for achieving your financial goals, but you have to make it a priority and live it. You need to understand that this plan is a living, breathing reality. Its purpose is to help give you a guideline for your year, but it can change. Life is unpredictable, and when we have changes, we need to adjust for them. I sit down with my clients every year, and we review and adapt their FitPlans. We reflect on how successful they were in following the previous year's plan and where they want to do things differently in the next year. We take into account their near- and long-term goals and where they are in their journey, and we incorporate all of this into their plan.

I AM NOW FINANCIALLY FIT!

Just as the process of getting physically fit is not an overnight one, the process of getting Financially Fit also requires commitment and patience. Based on your level of commitment to your plan, you will find that over the course of six months to a year, you will see tremendous results, and you will feel as though you are Financially Fit. By now, you have been focused on living a financially healthier lifestyle, and after focusing on the details, targeting problem areas, and committing to a financial fitness plan, you are starting to see results. The results that you are seeing are smaller credit card balances or lower debts and increased bank account balances. When you get to this place and feel that you have truly changed your past behaviors, then I think it is safe to say that you can call yourself Financially Fit. However, just because you are Financially Fit does not mean the process stops.

Just as with weight loss and staying physically fit, financial fitness is an ongoing effort that takes constant work and vigilance. As I mentioned in the introduction, certain sections will seem repetitive in this Financially Fit section; however, I have tailored this section to someone who was previously Financially Fat. I share this because even though you have achieved your financial goals, you have the potential to slip back into your past behaviors. Just as some people need to work harder at keeping weight off than others, Financially Skinny and Financially Fat people will have to work harder than intrinsically Financially Fit people until they have been practicing financial fitness long enough that it becomes part of their nature to consistently make financially fit choices. This is not a good or a bad thing; it is just a fact and something you should always keep in the back of your mind. Now that you are actively practicing Financially Fit habits, there are other areas of your financial life that can be put into focus.

USING CREDIT

As a Financially Fat person, you are likely not a stranger to credit. Through the process of becoming Financially Fit, you may have even grown to detest your credit cards as you realized that they created more problems for you and made it difficult to achieve your financial goals. When credit is not used wisely, it is absolutely a bad thing and you should detest it; however, there are many techniques and strategies for making credit a positive influence in your life. Hopefully, you have cleaned yours up if it was a problem and have not lost the ability to gain access to credit. Let's explore some smart strategies and benefits for utilizing credit.

INTEREST EARNED ON YOUR MONEY

Typically when you purchase something with credit, you have at least thirty days until you have to pay the credit card company. Take for example a $1,000 purchase. If you were going to pay cash for this item, the cash would come out of your checking account immediately. If you utilized a credit card, though, you would have an additional thirty days of this cash sitting in your bank account.

If your bank paid you 5 percent on your cash, and if you had $1,000 in the bank, this would amount to a little over $4 for the month. You may think that sounds like a small amount of money, but I bet if you found $4 on the street you would be excited about it. Why not find it in your own bank account? I always tell clients that interest paid to you by banks is "free money."

The relatively small size of the interest earned does not change the fact that it is free, and you should value it as such. If you are looking at a purchase of this size or larger from a store that offers free financing for a period of time, then the same rule applies. Plus, you get even more time to earn free money. If you were going to spend the same $1,000 and got free financing for twelve months, then this would mean that you had twelve months for your money to earn interest for you. At 5 percent, you are now looking at $50 for the year. Now imagine if you found $50 on the street!

These strategies obviously only work if you plan to pay the credit card company back before interest and penalties are charged on the credit cards. My clients make sure that they give themselves reminders with plenty of time before the due date so that they do not incur undue penalties due to this strategy. And remember, anything that you purchase with credit should be part of your FitPlan at this point.

POINTS/REWARDS AND CASH BACK

Many companies offer cards that give you points, rewards, or cash back on money that you spend on the card. This is another way that you can get free money, this time from the credit card company. Depending on the card, on average, you can expect to get 1 percent back on what you spend or 1 percent toward points or rewards.

Going back to the $1,000 purchase, this would mean for every $1,000 you spend, you would get a $10 value in either cash or rewards. If you were already planning on spending this money, then why not get rewarded for doing so?

There are many types of rewards cards, and I always advise clients to utilize the ones that would provide the most meaningful rewards. I have a client who only flies Southwest Airlines and likes to travel. So she utilizes the Southwest credit card, and her spending helps pay for her trips. Because she is earning points on money she was going to spend anyway, we can put it to work elsewhere at the same time. I have some clients who like to give money to charity, and there are a number of cards that will let you do just that.

I know a number of people who also take advantage of the signup bonus on rewards cards, where if you spend a certain amount of money on the card in a given period, you will be given extra rewards and points. This is a great strategy to utilize when you know you have a large impending purchase.

The only catch with rewards cards is the possibility of an annual fee, which is how many of these card companies fund their rewards programs. Depending on the rewards level, the fee may be reasonable. If your annual fee were $100, then you would be paying around $8 a month for the benefit of using this card. As long as your rewards are more than $8 a month, then the fee makes sense. So, if you spend $1,000 a month and get $10 back, $8 would go to the fee and $2 would be your truly free money.

If you cannot easily determine the annual fee on the rewards card, call the company and ask. Also, look for rewards cards with no annual fee as well, or for card companies that will give you the first year free.

IMPROVED CREDIT SCORE

As a Financially Fat person, you may or may not have good credit. It is important to grasp that using credit wisely actually improves your credit score. If you used credit poorly in the past, showing a change in behavior will look good for your credit score going forward. One of the strangest pieces of advice credit counseling companies give people with bad credit histories is to get more credit. What they are telling people is that they should show that they have changed and prove that they can use credit responsibly. Over a period of time, you will see improvements in your credit score. If you had good credit already, then you can continue to improve upon your score.

FLEXIBILITY IN CASE OF EMERGENCY

When you use credit, you free up your cash for other purposes, especially emergencies. Nowadays almost all merchants take credit cards for payment; however, these cannot always be used for everything. At the end of the day, cash is king, and it will remain so unless we have some global financial meltdown that forces us to start trading in gold, goods, and services again. Until that day, it is always wise to keep a responsible reserve of cash for emergencies.

It is important to note that when I mention using credit, I don't always mean credit cards. Let's look at the example of my wonderful friend who purchased his house with cash. He saved and worked hard for years to build up enough money to pay for his house and closing costs. The only problem with this strategy is that after he closed, he realized that his home needed some substantial repairs, and he did not have enough cash left in his reserves to pay for them. He ultimately was able to obtain a home equity line on his home to cover these repairs. The good news for him is that, similar to a mortgage, he is able to deduct the interest he pays on his home equity line of credit from his tax return. The bad news is that he has less overall credit available (home equity lines are typically smaller than mortgages), and he has the possibility of paying more interest over time, depending on the type of home equity line he utilized.

As I frequently tell clients that their financial journey is a long one, and despite all of the planning you can do, you never know what unexpected situations can arise. Like a spare tire, a cash reserve is the best way to plan for those unexpected events on your life's journey. The optimal size of your cash reserve depends on many factors. When I have clients who intend to buy a home, we plan on a cash reserve for their down payment and closing costs, but I always make sure that they have four to six months of mortgage payments reserved and another reserve for repairs, especially if they are buying an older home. No matter how great your home inspector is or how reliable you think the previous owners are, you never know what issues may be lurking in your "used" home.

A bank or mortgage provider requires you to have enough cash for the down payment and closing costs, but they do not demand that you have cash beyond those figures (they primarily look at your income as an indicator of repayment after closing). Remember, a bank or mortgage company is just a pit stop on your journey through life, and they are not really concerned with you beyond that one initial stop. I want to see you have the ability to make *all* of the stops you would like to make.

There are many opinions on how to manage the types of credit that you have, and I encourage you to constantly compare what interest rates you are paying across these types of credit options. I sometimes see clients with balances on credit cards with interest rates of 15–20 percent; however, they have or could have a home equity line of credit that they could utilize to pay down the credit cards and pay less than 6 percent. On $10,000, this could save you $900 a year. Using credit like mortgages, credit cards, or home equity lines may cause you some interest payments that you did not want to make. However, they give you more freedom with your cash, which could be worth more than that down the road.

USE YOUR CREDIT CARD MORE

Whether you had a problem in the past or you have managed your credit well, I challenge you to start using it more. Think about the times when you use your debit card or pay with a check and determine whether you can change your payment method to a credit card. For every time that you use the card, keep your receipt and do not pay the card right away. Wait until your credit card payment date and then pay the bill. If you make a practice of this strategy and it becomes part of your routine, you will earn more money in your checking or savings accounts, and you can earn points and rewards depending on your card type.

INVESTING WISELY

Now that you have been saving more money, focusing on your investments should become more of a priority. Many people who have not had money to invest before are unsure what to do or may not want to take any risks, as they have worked so hard to even have money to invest.

I have mentioned before that I became disillusioned with the attempt to predict the performance of financial markets while I worked at the wealth management firm, but I still find value in them. I believe that over time, and with a well-diversified portfolio that is rebalanced at least once a year, you can achieve 6–8 percent returns. There are risks to achieving this performance; however, I feel that it is a good and achievable estimate.

Those of us who had money invested in stocks from 2000 to 2012 find it difficult to believe that there is much value in the financial markets. And when you look at stocks over this period of time, that assessment is pretty much true. The stock market was basically flat during this time, meaning that if you invested $100 in 2000, you would have $100 in 2012. Some people reading this may even have lost money in the markets at this time. There were a number of significant drops in stocks, but there were significant gains as well. The issue with performance in people's investment portfolios over this period of time was not the fact that they were invested in stocks; it is that they were invested in *too much* stock and not in enough other investments.

While stocks did not perform well in recent years, the bond market did. If you have a well-diversified portfolio, meaning you invested in stocks *and* bonds, then you had better returns than someone who did not.

When you make any investment with your money, there are always risks; however, it is important to understand the types of money you have and what is appropriate for each money type. I always tell my clients that they have three buckets of money: cash, "moon" money, and "life" money.

Cash is the money that you might need for living expenses within the next six months to a year (depending on how conservative you are) should any catastrophic life event happen, such as a job loss or death of a spouse. Cash should typically be kept in a bank, savings account, or money market mutual fund: very conservative investments that are available to you daily. You want to take minimal risk with this money, as it represents your emergency funds.

Moon money represents the funds that you will need to draw during retirement. I call it moon money because if you are under 59½ years old or more than ten years from retirement, this is money that you should not touch. When you think of accessing it, consider it as easy to reach as the moon. Moon money should be invested the most aggressively. You have time until your retirement, so these funds can fluctuate up and down with the markets. Over time, they will make you more money than your bank account, despite the fact that sometimes it does not feel like it.

That leaves us with life money. This is the money that you have saved that allows you to live the life you want by doing things like buying a home or going on vacation. This money gives you the most flexibility to live your life. And many clients, especially Fit people, believe that this money should be treated as cash and exposed to no risk whatsoever. I understand this thought process. This is the money that is reserved for "life," and no one wants his or her life to be at risk. However, if you do not plan to utilize this money in the next two to five years, then it should not be sitting in a checking account. It should not be invested as aggressively as the moon money, but it should be invested in something more aggressive than a bank account. As the time comes closer to using the money, it should be moved into the cash bucket. Until then, it should be working for you by earning interest or growing in value.

I had clients who kept a significant amount of money (greater than $50,000) in a checking account. They only needed a small portion of this money for cash and emergencies; therefore, we invested the remainder into bond funds. These are more risky than a bank account and could lose value on any given day; however, over a period of two to five years, they will earn more money than in a bank account.

Depending on how long and how well you have been practicing good financial health, you may or may not have enough saved to have three buckets. You may just have enough for one, the cash bucket. But as you continue on your path and become more and more Financially Fit, you will have enough for three buckets. You should remember that each bucket should be progressively riskier. When you separate the three and invest wisely, your buckets will grow over time, with minimal effort on your part.

BUCKETS

Reserve some time in your calendar to review your money and where you have it invested or deposited. Look at the total picture and determine whether you have three buckets (cash, life money, and moon or retirement money) or just one or two. If you have fewer than three, determine which bucket needs more. If you have three buckets, review what they are invested in. If they are too conservative, think about ways to take on more risk. You can speak to a financial adviser or consult with any number of financial websites like ETrade, Fidelity, Vanguard, or Charles Schwab.

INVESTMENTS

If you realized that your investments in your life or moon buckets are too conservative, you need to take some time to educate yourself on taking proper investment risk. Most of my clients who are not investing as much as they should are typically not doing it because they are afraid of the unknown; they have not had enough education on investing. I know that for some people, investing money seems incredibly scary and complicated—I was one of those people. However, with some education and practice, it really is not that scary. The first resource I tell clients to utilize is their own investment firm. If you already have a retirement account or brokerage account with ETrade, Fidelity, or any other firm, you should feel free to use their resources. After all, your balances are making them money, so you should feel free to benefit in return. Many of these websites have great online classes and tutorials, or you can always call their 800 numbers and speak to an adviser. If you choose to speak with an adviser, make sure that the adviser explains concepts to you until you understand them. I hate to see people invest in things and not fully understand them because they were afraid to ask questions. Ask lots of questions! It's your money, and you deserve to feel completely comfortable with what you do with it.

I also think there are a number of great blogs out there that explain investing in a very useful manner; you will discover many just by searching "finance blogs." I have recently started a YouTube channel where I discuss various investment topics, and I encourage you to check it out.

Just as it takes time to get physically fit, it takes time to gain an understanding of investments; however, it is time that is very well spent, in my opinion. I encourage you to dedicate time to finding the investment resources that most appeal to you, and spend some time each week reviewing them. Once you have gone through the exercise of determining your money buckets and how much should be put in each, it will be a matter of determining the best asset allocation for each bucket. When you are researching your investment options, look for those that will meet your asset allocation needs. Generally speaking, your cash bucket options should have a conservative asset allocation, your life bucket options should be moderately conservative to moderate, and your moon bucket options should be moderately aggressive to aggressive. Knowing your appropriate asset allocation actually makes the selection of investments a much easier process. And again, many of the financial websites provide guidance on what asset allocation might be best for you, based on your life goals.

CHAPTER 6

What Every Financial Type Needs for Success

Whether or not you currently have Financially Fit habits, I believe that everyone needs a financial road map for life. Having an idea of where you are and where you are headed takes a great deal of stress out of your life. The construction of this road map can be executed by going through the "Life's Journey" exercise at the beginning of the book; the fine details would be accomplished through a fitness plan. As I mentioned before, I advise my clients to review this exercise at least once a year. This may seem tedious; however, this is your financial health and well-being that we are talking about, and I do not think that we could ever spend too much time on it.

I find that this road map exercise is especially important for my clients who are married or in a long-term committed relationship. Having a clear and agreed-upon path for where you want to go in life relieves stress in relationships. If you have a Financially Fit person and a Financially Fat person in a relationship, for example, they typically face many challenges emerging from their financial practices. But if they can sit down and agree on specific financial goals every year, then they know they are working toward something together, and they become more of a team.

I recently experienced this with a couple I met. They wanted to buy a house and achieve a certain lifestyle when they retired. The husband, however, had a spending problem, and they couldn't seem to get ahead. When we discussed that the house and retirement goals would be in jeopardy because of his financial health, the reality hit home. Now his wife did not have to nag him about his spending; they had a common goal, and they both needed to work together to achieve it.

I know that we are all different and some of us prefer to fly by the seat of our pants more than others; if you are one of these people, I urge you to leave that philosophy for other areas of your life and commit to a road map when it comes to your financial life. There is nothing worse for me as a planner than to sit down with people, ask them their goals, and realize that they have never thought about this—or worse, that they are unable to accomplish their goals because of their past behaviors. As I mentioned before, if you are going on a 3,000-mile road trip, doesn't it make sense to use a map or GPS? As with a travel map, the financial road map ensures that you will take the most efficient trip while also accomplishing as much as possible along the way.

CONSTANT REVIEW OF THE ROAD MAP

Hopefully you will commit to creating a road map for your financial life. However, it is not just enough to create it; you need to review it with some frequency. I advise clients to informally review their road map once a quarter and to do a full review and/or restructuring once a year. I believe that this review is one of the most critical keys to long-term financial health and success. Your life is constantly evolving and changing as you head toward retirement, and you want to make sure that you are on the right path. If your path has changed, you need to adjust your life accordingly.

I have clients who put together a financial plan after they got married. Like most people, they never reviewed it, but they felt comfortable with the fact that they at least went through the exercise. Then the clients decided to have a baby. The child was not part of the initial financial plan, and they never revisited that plan. What happened to this couple is what happens to many people: They had the child, but never changed their spending and saving habits. They came to see me when the child was five, and their financial health had deteriorated dramatically over those five years. They did not know how it happened, but they knew that they had gotten off track somehow.

We have since put together a new plan, and now they are back on the road and in good shape. If they had been reviewing and revising their plan every year, though, they would not have gotten so far behind on their goals. What is the point of plotting out your trip with GPS or a road map if you are not going to review it to see where you are? Once you stop looking, you could easily get lost and end up somewhere you did not intend. Even if you feel that not much has happened to you over a period of three months or a year, you should still go through the exercise of reviewing your plan. Sometimes small changes can make a bigger impact than you think.

COMMITMENT TO YOURSELF

Financial fitness and health matter as much as your physical health. Just as I believe you should commit to keeping yourself physically healthy, I believe you need to commit to keeping yourself financially healthy.

This commitment is easier for some than others. If you are a Financially Skinny or Fat person, this will be a difficult task for you; however, it is a necessary one. One of the reasons I left the wealth management firm to start my own company is that I saw firsthand how critical it was to implement sound financial practices in life as early as possible. When I would meet with younger people, teach them best practices, and have them commit, the results were dramatic and exciting. On the other hand, it was always difficult to meet with older clients who had hopes and dreams that they still wanted to accomplish, but have to tell them that they couldn't, because their financial health was so poor due to years of bad habits. It was still difficult for them to change, despite my efforts, because they had spent years building those bad habits. It is not impossible for these people to change, but just as it gets harder to lose weight as you grow older, it is harder to practice healthy financial habits as well.

No matter what age or financial fitness type you are, though, I truly hope that you make a commitment to becoming financially healthy and fit. I want you to achieve every goal possible in life, and the secret to being able to accomplish those goals is financial fitness. Good luck on your journey, and enjoy the ride!

APPENDIX

Exercises for Every Fitness Type

VISUALIZING YOUR JOURNEY

As a planner for my clients, when I first meet with them, I share the following thoughts. Your adult life is like a road trip from New York to California. New York is where you are when you are just starting out, and California is retirement. I view my role as the person who is responsible for helping them get to California:

1. in the time they want to get there;

2. living in the house they want to live in when they get there;

3. making all of the stops they want to make along the way.

When I meet people, they are not always in New York. Sometimes people are in Ohio or Colorado. One of my clients said she felt she was in Maine, because her $200,000 in student loan debt had set her back in life. It is not necessarily critical for you to figure out what state you are in. What is more critical at this point is determining what your road trip looks like.

Take five to ten minutes to sit quietly. Close your eyes. Take a few deep breaths, and think about what you want out of life. Take a pen and paper and write these things down.

What is important to you?

1. Do you want to have a career?
2. Do you want to get married?
3. Do you want to have children?
4. Do you want to be a stay-at-home mom/dad?
5. Do you want to retire by a certain age?
6. Do you want to get a college degree, or another degree?
7. Do you want to buy a house?

What are bucket list items that you absolutely have to do before you die?

1. Do you want to travel internationally?
2. Do you want to skydive?
3. Do you want to give to charity?
4. Do you want to go skiing/hiking/mountain climbing/surfing?

These first two lists should be considered your "needs" in life and the items that you prioritize when planning.

What are everyday things that you feel you need to be happy?

This list is more of the "wants" you have in life. It is not as critical as the first two, but it would be nice to have these things if you could.

1. Do you like to eat out?

2. Do you like lattes five times a week or more?

3. Do you like to go out with friends multiple times a week?

4. Do you like to go shopping multiple times a month?

FINANCIALLY FIT EXERCISES

SPENDING MONEY

Sit down and think of two ways you can spend money. The first is on something for you. You do not have to go crazy, but think about something you have always wanted to do—and do it! The other involves doing something for someone else. Think about a way you can surprise a person you love with a long-desired thing or experience. For my clients who have spending goals such as these, we usually set up a separate savings account for "fun" money. Some clients determine in advance how much fun money they will need and make a specific savings objective for it. For example, if they want to take a trip and the trip costs $500, they plan to put $42 a month in this account so that after a year, they will have the $500 saved. Other clients use this account for leftover money they have at the end of the month. They know that it is not earmarked for any emergencies or necessities, so if they want to use the money for fun, they have available whatever is in that account. The fun money account is a great method for spending money while not feeling bad about it. My clients like knowing that they have planned for fun.

USE YOUR CREDIT CARD MORE

If you are someone who *rarely* uses your credit card, I challenge you to start using it more. For every time you use the card, keep your receipt and do not pay the card right away. Wait until your credit card payment date and then pay the bill. If you make a practice of this strategy and it becomes part of your routine, you will earn more money in your checking or savings accounts, and you can earn points and rewards depending on your card type.

BUCKETS

Reserve some time in your calendar to review your money and where you have it invested or deposited. Look at the total picture and determine whether you have three buckets or just one or two. If you have fewer than three, determine which bucket needs more. If you have three buckets, review what they are invested in. If they are too conservative, think about ways to take on more risk. You can speak to a financial adviser or consult with any number of financial websites like Fidelity, Vanguard, or Charles Schwab.

INVESTMENTS

If you realized that the investments in your life or moon buckets are too conservative, you need to take some time to educate yourself on taking proper investment risk. Most of my clients who are not investing as much as they should are typically not doing it because they are afraid of the unknown. They have not had enough education on investing.

I know that for some people, investing money seems incredibly scary and complicated——I was one of those people. However, with some education and practice, it really is not that painful. The first resource I tell clients to utilize is their own investment firm. If you already have a retirement account or brokerage account with ETrade, Fidelity, or any other firm, you should feel free to use their resources. After all, your balances are making them money, so you should feel free to benefit in return. Many of these websites have great online classes and tutorials, or you can always call their 800 numbers and speak to an adviser. If you choose to speak with an adviser, make sure that this person explains concepts to you until you understand them. I hate to see people invest in things and not fully understand them because they were afraid to ask questions. Ask lots of questions! It's your money, and you deserve to feel completely comfortable with what you do with it.

There are also a number of great blogs out there that explain investing in a very useful manner. Just by searching "finance blogs," you will discover quite a number. I have recently started a YouTube channel where I discuss various investment topics. I encourage you to check it out.

Just as it takes time to get physically fit, it takes time to gain an understanding of investments; however, it is time that is very well spent, in my opinion. I encourage you to dedicate time to finding the investment resources that most appeal to you and then spending some time each week reviewing them. Once you have gone through the exercise of determining your money buckets and how much should be put in each, it will be a matter of determining the best asset allocation for each bucket. When you are researching your investment options, look for those that will meet your asset allocation needs. Generally speaking, your cash bucket options should have a conservative asset allocation, your life bucket options should be moderately conservative to moderate, and your moon bucket options should be moderately aggressive to aggressive. Knowing your appropriate asset allocation actually makes the selection of investments a much easier process. And again, many financial websites provide guidance on what asset allocation might be best for you, based on your life goals.

FINANCIALLY SKINNY EXERCISES

USING THE FINE-TOOTH COMB

Print out three to four months of credit and debit card statements. Yes, print them out! I find that people are able to analyze information better when it is in print. Then look at the expenses in order of size value and categorize them by high, medium, and low costs. Next, look at the frequency of each purchase. Do you see multiple charges for one location? Do you see daily or weekly charges for something? Is this a good thing or a bad thing?

NEEDS, WANTS, WASTES

Review your spending from the last three to four months and try to place every dollar spent into one of these categories. If you have everything listed as a need, then you should go back and look at each item more objectively or ask for help in categorizing everything. Look at your wastes and add them up. How much could you have saved in three to four months if you had avoided wastes? Are there wants or wastes that can be eliminated or adjusted?

TARGET AND ATTACK PROBLEM AREAS

If you have determined any problem areas above, write them down and strategize how to eliminate or work on them. Consider whether each is a problem because of the frequency of purchases, the size of purchases, or both. Do you need to go to Starbucks every day? Can you replace one of those Starbucks trips with coffee from home or a cart on the street? Are you going to J. Crew or any retail store too much? Determine why you are frequenting the store. Is it because it is on your way home? Can you plan a different way home? Can you walk into the store, find things you would want to buy, write down the prices, and simply walk out?

SPENDING——*STOP* AND *WHY*

Most people at various times in their life have spending problems. Some of us have it worse than others. I had a *very* bad spending problem, which stemmed from making good money and having credit. I always told myself there would be more money down the road, so I could put purchases on my credit card. I *never* thought there would be an end to the money. However, when I wanted to make a career change that would provide me less money but more fulfillment, I realized that I needed to control my spending. The basic tenets of financial health are earning more and spending less. If you cannot earn more, then you need to spend less. This exercise is the most valuable one for my clients to help them with their spending, and you can do it *every single day.* Every time that you are about to spend money, STOP yourself for a brief minute and ask, WHY? Why are you buying what you are buying?

The great news for you is that there are only two correct answers to this question: (1) It is life and death. You will literally die if you don't buy health insurance or a medication or take a trip to the emergency room; (2) you have planned for it. If you made that purchase of the new phone or the clothes for work part of your plan for the year, then you can go ahead and buy that item. If one of these two answers was not applicable, put down that item, walk away, and don't look back.

THE FOLLOW-UP TO *STOP* AND *WHY*

So you have just practiced the STOP and WHY exercise, and you feel bad. You typically feel good buying things and spending money, and you *really* wanted to spend the money you were just going to—but instead you practiced a financial fitness exercise, and now you feel bad. Now what? When you experience this level of sadness for not making a purchase, find a new outlet for the displaced happiness.

When I was losing weight, I really wanted to eat a cheeseburger, and eating a salad just didn't feel as good. So I would eat the salad and visual-ize the way it would make me look. Or I would let myself have the salad with a small treat like a glass of wine or a piece of candy. Similarly, the thing you were just about to buy was not part of your plan, but is there something else that is? Can you buy that instead?

You can also try distracting yourself with something that makes you happy. Call a friend, play an app on your phone, go for a walk. Try a number of different distracting exercises so that you do not fixate on the fact that you felt bad that you did not make that purchase. You do not want to feel as though you are deprived or missing out while you are on the road to finan-cial fitness. If you do, then you are less likely to stay on this important path.

NO-SPEND DAYS

Another way to prevent yourself from having a spending issue is to com-mit to achieving a certain number of no-spend days a month. During a no-spend day, you literally will plan to not use your cash or debit and credit cards for an entire day. It is a best practice to plan one of these a week, and an easy way to accomplish this exercise is just to take your driver's license out with you and leave the rest of your wallet home for the day. While you are practicing a no-spend day, make sure you reflect on where you would have spent money if you could have spent money. This is another great way for you to identify problem areas in your spending life.

CASH-ONLY DAYS

Similar to no-spend days, I think it is a best practice to have at least one cash-only day a week. The set amount of cash you allow yourself to spend during the day should be a difficult goal for you, and for most clients this number is usually around $20. Think of cash-only days like "push days" when you are working out at the gym. Maybe you can easily run two miles at a time, but on a push day, you make yourself run three. Maybe you normally spend $40 a day on various items, so push yourself once a week to only spend $20.

ENVELOPE SYSTEM

A number of my clients have a difficult time understanding how much money they are spending, because they typically use credit cards more than they should. Or they will go through the process of creating their FitPlan, but have a difficult time tracking it because they are using credit and debit cards and do not always update their monitoring system. A great solution for these issues is creating envelopes for the funds that you allocated through your FitPlan. If you designated $200 a month for food, then you should take out $200 once a month and put this in your food envelope, and only use the funds from this envelope to pay for food. If you are getting close to the end of the month and there is not much cash in the envelope, then you will know that you have to eat what you have on hand or make different plans. I would encourage you to create an envelope for as many categories on your FitPlan as possible. Then you should also create a "fun" envelope. You can use this envelope to hold the funds that remain in the other envelopes at the end of the month. This is your reward for responsible planning during the month.

FINANCIALLY FAT EXERCISES

ACKNOWLEDGING THAT YOU ARE FINANCIALLY FAT

You either knew already that you are Financially Fat, or you didn't realize it until you took my quiz. Take a few minutes and think about your financial life to date. What do you think led you to become Financially Fat? Are you an overspender? Do you use too many credit cards? Do you spend too much time shopping? Do you go out too much? Come up with a list of five reasons why you are Financially Fat. Write them down. Keep this list to refer back to as you go through this process. I am a big proponent of letting things go and moving forward, and this list is the beginning of you letting go of your past life of financial fatness and moving forward into financial fitness.

PATIENCE

Visualize what financial fitness looks like to you. Is it lower credit? Is it more savings? Is it financial freedom (i.e., the ability to do what you want when you want)? Create a distinct image of what this looks like. If you have words for it, then write them down. If they are more like images, then save them to your phone, a Pinterest page, or print them out. There will be times when you feel that you are not achieving your success as rapidly as you would like, and when you feel like that, refer to these words or images. Keep them as your motivation. This is akin to keeping your "eyes on the prize." It always helps to have a written or visual representation of what the prize is, and this will be yours.

PROBLEM MINIMIZATION

I gave a few examples in the book of ways to combat your problem areas. Now I challenge you to brainstorm more ways you can minimize them. Do you need to remove the problem completely, as in the case of the too-expensive apartment? Will visualization help you? Is there something equally as fun, just different and less expensive, that you can replace this with? As you implement this plan, start tracking how much you are saving by having the strategy in place (for example, if you go into a store, figure out how much you would have spent if you weren't combating your shopping habit). Keeping an ongoing tally of these numbers helps make your success even more profound, as you not only have saved yourself the money, but you kept yourself from going more into debt at the same time.

YOUR REWARD CHART

Take the time out of your schedule to create a reward chart for yourself. Think about what your short- and long-term financial goals are and how you should reward yourself for achieving them. You can make this in Excel and add pictures or photos. If you are new to the financial fitness process, you can start with one or two easy goals, but as you do this for longer, you should challenge yourself to achieve more difficult goals. An example of a short-term goal is not using your credit card for a month, or spending only a certain amount of money a week, or paying down a certain amount of your student loans or credit cards. The goal should be achievable within a month, and at the end of the month, if you have accomplished this, give yourself a small reward. This could be an iTunes gift card, an extra cocktail when you go out, or a new pair of earrings. An example of a long-term goal is something that you could accomplish within six months to a year. It could be the same as the short-term goal, only larger in size. If you accomplish this goal, you should have a bigger reward. This could be a new purse, a fancy dinner, or a nice bottle of wine. Please keep in mind that your rewards should not create additional financial burdens on you, so keep them appropriately sized, given your goals.

WITH A LITTLE HELP FROM MY FRIENDS

Think about a friend or a group of friends that you hang out with frequently, and during an appropriate get-together, share with this group your struggles with your finances and how you plan to change this about yourself. Ask for their help or suggestions for ways you can save money and spend less. I have a client who is in a book club with a few women, and the book club decided to work together to brainstorm different ways they could all save money collectively. If you have a group of friends that meets once a week for cocktails, see if they are open to "nights in" where the goal is to spend the least amount of money but have the maximum amount of fun. Instead of shopping trips, try walking or hiking with a friend. I have another client who has made it a competition with her friend to see who can save the most (on a percentage basis) over a six-month period, and the loser has to buy dinner for the winner. See how many people you can enlist to join you on the road to financial fitness.

SELF-MONITORING

Schedule a weekly meeting with yourself to look over your finances for the first three months of financial fitness training. After that, schedule a monthly meeting. Spend at least one hour of your time looking over your numbers. Examine your reward chart. Are you on target? Have you cleared your hurdles? Are you doing the appropriate exercises? Did you have a setback? How can you correct this problem? Are your friends helping or hurting your progress?

ACKNOWLEDGMENTS

You always hear the expression, "Behind every great man there is a great woman." Well, the reverse is true in my house. If you consider me a great woman, it is only because I have the support of a great man. My husband Bill has been my best friend, my biggest cheerleader, my bunker buddy, and my constant supporter for more than a decade. I do not make it easy on him, but his love has truly given me the energy and wings that I use to soar to great heights, and I thank him for giving it freely and unconditionally. The other great man in my life is my little man, my son Will. I always tell people that loving him makes me a better person, and I think that is the greatest compliment I can give him. I would also like to say that he is one of the most Financially Fit people that I know.

Most people only have two parents, but I have been fortunate to have four. I am especially grateful for a dad whose tough love made me constantly strive to succeed and a mom whose unconditional love gave me a safety net in case I fell short of those goals. In addition to having four parents, I have six siblings who have all challenged me and inspired me my entire life. I love you all immensely. When I married Bill, I gained another three parents to add to my four and two siblings to add to my six. They have never felt like "in-laws," and I am grateful for their love and support of our family.

I have had some amazing bosses and mentors in my life, but one of the greatest would have to be Michael Simonds. I will be eternally grateful to him for believing in me when literally no one else would. He took a chance, called in a chip on my behalf, and *always* had my back from that point on. I not only have a large immediate family, but also a greater extended network of family and friends, and I thank them for their support. It is always nice to know that they are there cheering for my successes, but ready to pick me up if I fail. There are many friends that I would like to thank personally; however, for purposes of time and space I will just name a few here and hopefully name more in future books. A very large "thank you" goes to Dr. Scott Boehnen. He not only makes one of the best apple pies you can imagine and provides excellent dinner conversation, but he is also a great book editor. Another wonderfully talented editor and friend is Anne Taylor. Thank you both for generously devoting your time to this book. Finally, I would also like to thank Timothy Tosta, a friend and life coach. He truly helped save my life many years ago, and his practices and teachings are a large part of my work today.

CPSIA information can be obtained at www.ICGtesting.com
Printed in the USA
BVOW07s1854250914

368384BV00001B/4/P